Words Aptly Spoken®
BRITISH LITERATURE
a companion guide to classic literature

SECOND EDITION

compiled and edited by Jen Greenholt

MULTIMEDIA

Jen Greenholt, *Words Aptly Spoken®* Series
A Companion Guide to Classic Literature, British Literature
First edition published 2008. Second edition published 2011.

©2011 Classical Conversations® MultiMedia. All rights reserved.

Published by Classical Conversations, Inc.
255 Air Tool Drive
Southern Pines, NC 28387
www.ClassicalConversations.com | www.ClassicalConversationsBooks.com

Cover design by Classical Conversations. Cover image from *The Writings of Charles Dickens*, frontispiece, public domain.

Printed in the United States of America.

ISBN: 978-0-9829845-2-9

Acknowledgments

Many thanks to the members of Classical Conversations, who have made this book possible. Special thanks to the editors, who catch my mistakes and add the polish to make this book the best it can be.

Foreword

This collection introduces you to twenty classic works of British literature, beginning with Anglo-Saxon poetry and carrying you into the twentieth century.

To help you navigate the literature, *Words Aptly Spoken: British Literature* will lead you through an overview of literary genres and devices. The collection opens with a discussion of literary techniques and a glossary of some common terms used to talk about literature. These terms appear in **boldface** in the main text, and they are defined and used in a sentence in the introductory glossary.

As with the other collections in the *Words Aptly Spoken* series, *British Literature* contains a series of questions about each work. Review Questions ensure that you understand the basic plot, characters, setting, and message of the book. Thought Questions take the themes and ideas raised by each author and help you apply them to other, more familiar situations.

The complexity of British literature makes it a perfect setting in which to further practice and refine your writing skills. This collection also includes writing practice sections that will encourage you to strengthen your analytical and critical writing skills.

Before the questions devoted to each book, there will be a short section entitled "Understanding Literature." That section will give you background information on the book's genre and some of the devices it uses. Be on the lookout for those characteristics as you read. You may be asked to use the new information in the "Writing Refinement" section after the questions.

These works of British literature are adult-level reading. By this time, you should be able to read closely for details and plot, so the Review and Thought Questions will focus on the major themes and concepts of the books.

All this being said, take a deep breath and get ready to plunge into some great works of British literature.

Best wishes and happy reading!

Table of Contents

A Note for Parents: Tools for the Journey

If you have ever heard Shakespeare performed before a live audience and marveled at the ease with which the words flowed from the actors' lips; if you have ever envied people who can call on Milton, Dickens, Joyce, and Lewis to lend eloquence to their argument; if you have skimmed a list of the hundred greatest novels of all time and winced as you remembered struggling to finish *The Grapes of Wrath* in high school—you may think that the great conversations of literature are forever closed to you. The good news is—they're not!

Whether you are a student, an adult, a parent, a child, or all of the above, you have the capability to train yourself not only to read great literature, but also to share its beauty, truth, and joy with others.

Although most people learn to read as children, the art of deliberately engaging with the content and ideas of a novel or short story requires ongoing practice.

The *Words Aptly Spoken* series is based on the classical model of education,[1] which breaks learning into three natural stages: grammar, dialectic, and rhetoric. In the grammar stage, you learn the vocabulary of a subject. In the dialectic stage, you learn to develop logical arguments and analyze others' ideas. In the rhetoric stage, you explore the consequences of ideas as you form and express your own. This guide will help you as you begin to apply the classical model to the study of literature.

Why British Literature?

In British literature you will find a subtle, often dry sense of humor, a deep interest in politics and social issues, and an equally strong appreciation for the romantic, the absurd, and the mysterious. Each of the works included in this collection has influenced popular culture and the literature that has come after it. Take Bunyan's *The Pilgrim's Progress*: written in the 1670s, it was rewritten in the nineteenth century by Nathaniel Hawthorne as a short story, "The Celestial Railroad," and revisited by C.S. Lewis as *The Pilgrim's Regress* in the 1950s.

Although the messages of these books are obviously powerful, one aim of this collection is to make you aware of them as books—works created using specific tools to achieve both deliberate and unintentional effects. Thinking about literature this way should not hurt your ability to simply enjoy a good book. Rather, it should add another dimension to the mystery, romance, thrill, or delight an author creates using words on a page.

How to Use This Book

Despite popular belief, reading is not wholly instinctive. Because comprehension, analysis, and critical thinking require practice, each work of literature you will study is broken down by chapter into a series of questions designed to give structure and guidance to your reading.

Although the questions are arranged chapter-by-chapter, most readers will not pause to answer questions after finishing a chapter. If the book has captured your imagination the

---

[1] See Dorothy Sayers' essay, "The Lost Tools of Learning."

way classic literature ought to, you won't want to stop reading! For this reason, treat these questions as tools not only for reading, but also for writing, leading discussion, and sharing your ideas with others.

Review Questions pull out the **grammar** for each chapter: Who is the book about? (Characters) What happens? (Plot) Where does it take place? (Setting) What is the message? (Theme) What is the scope or time frame? (Focus) For readers of all ages, repeatedly asking these questions will generate good reading habits; eventually, as you read, your brain will automatically take note of this information and store it for future use.

Thought Questions are an exercise in **dialectic**, taking the basic elements from the Review Questions and encouraging you to analyze that information in light of other knowledge. As you become more familiar with the building blocks of a story, you should begin to ask questions of your own. What does this mean for me? How should I respond to this argument? You can use the Thought Questions to jump-start your own thinking process, as training tools for leading discussion, or as topics for essays.

If you cannot answer some of the questions by the time you have finished the book, consider going back and re-reading sections you may only have skimmed the first time. A word of caution: don't merely "look up" the answers to the questions and skim the rest of the book. Once established, this habit will make it harder for you to read and understand more difficult books. After all, self-respecting Olympic runners know that they would be at a severe disadvantage in the actual games if they secretly completed only half of their daily training regimen. In the same way, the results you achieve as a reader will reflect the quality and consistency of your training.

This collection emphasizes the grammar, or vocabulary, of literary study. Using specific terms allows you to discuss literature clearly and precisely, so keep your eyes out for **boldface** terms, which indicate a word with a specific meaning in relation to literature. Definitions can be found in the glossary at the end of the section on Devices and Conventions.

Because measuring progress is a part of learning, each section in this book begins or ends with suggested reading and writing exercises that allow you to gauge how well you have mastered the skills you've been practicing. Although exercises are suggested for each book, you can rearrange and revise to suit your needs.

The Journey in Perspective

One of the most important things to remember as you start—or resume—this journey is that it doesn't happen overnight. The art of leading and sharing in conversations about classical literature takes a lifetime to refine. You must begin with the fundamentals: learning to read closely, taking notes, and developing the vocabulary to structure your ideas and explain them to others (**grammar**). You must practice: adding new techniques, revising old ones, and comparing the results (**dialectic**). And then you will be ready to start all over again as you share the joy of the journey with others around you (**rhetoric**). Let's get started!

Reading Skills

Being a good reader takes practice, and it is vital to a range of other skills. If you miss the big ideas when you read, you cannot analyze or critique those ideas, identify the underlying messages, or respond to them thoughtfully in writing or conversation. These tips will help you read more effectively.

Vocabulary

If you see an unfamiliar word, take a minute to look up the definition and write it down. Not only will this improve your vocabulary, but it will help you avoid missing important details. Pay particular attention to words that have a different connotation now than they had when the book was written.

Characters

Keep a list of the main characters. Write down their names, a few defining characteristics, and their relationships with other characters. If you find a section that shows their character traits especially well, write down the page number.

Plot

Write down a skeletal outline of the book's plot. What happened, to whom, when, where, and how? Focus on turning points and revelations that were important to the plot's development.

Timeline

Keep a timeline of the major events in the book. This is especially useful if multiple subplots take place at the same time. You can also use a timeline to keep track of flashbacks or dream sequences.

Themes

Do you see a pattern in the problems that plague the characters? Is there some flaw that all the main characters share? Write it down. Also, if something in the book reminds you of another book or story you have read, jot down the page number(s) and the element(s) that seem similar.

Quotes

Does a character say something memorable? Underline or highlight it, or write down the page number and a few key words. When you write about or discuss the book, you will need evidence, and it is much easier to mark quotes as you go than to relocate specific passages when you need them.

Don't forget to read with a notebook or pad of sticky notes handy. If you own the book, margins are a great place to write, but make sure you use a bookmark so you can find your notes. Keep practicing these reading skills, and you will find your jobs as thinker, critic, and writer much easier as a result.

UNDERSTANDING LITERATURE: *Genres*

If you have ever seen a film adaptation of a book, you know that there is a marked difference between the two genres. Film versions rely heavily on action sequences and may extend battle or chase sequences beyond the scope of the book. Long passages of description must be recreated in visual form to the best of the director's ability. Dialogue is trimmed and patched to give it dramatic weight.

The reason for all these changes is that each genre has a different purpose, a different audience, and different conventions. Film, a visual medium, needs to capture the viewer's attention. Viewers cannot "put down" a movie at a theater. At home, if they turn it off, they are less likely to finish it later.

Books, on the other hand, can be read at one sitting or in chunks. The reader has to have enough description to create a mental picture of the story. If the author chooses, the reader can "see" the characters' inner thoughts and motivations but needs to be told about facial expressions or nervous twitches that an actor can portray on camera. Long action sequences may be hard to visualize in written form.

Just as there are different genres of media, there are also different genres within literature. Each one has certain conventions. Each one shares some characteristics with others, and each one is most effective for certain types of stories. It is important to recognize the strengths and weaknesses of different genres and to be able to evaluate how well an author utilizes his or her genre of choice.

Although it is important to remember that every work is distinct and may not fit neatly into one box, three broad, generally recognized categories of literature are poetry, drama, and prose.

Poetry

Poetry is one of the oldest recognized types of literature. Poetry is difficult to define because there are so many different types and styles, but a few general characteristics apply to most poems: 1) lines of poetry or verse are generally more compressed than lines of prose; 2) poetry has some type of internal structure, whether length of line, rhyme, meter, alliteration, or another device; and 3) poetry uses **symbolism** and imagery like **metaphors** and **similes** to create a a specific impression or image from each element in the poem.

Poems may be long or short, telling a story that takes place over fifty years or describing a single moment. Some poetry has a very strict form, in which the end of every line **rhymes** with the next one. Poetry can also have no rhyme at all. For example, **blank verse** has no rhymes, but it still has **meter**, or a regular number of accented syllables per line. **Free verse** does not have regular meter.

Styles of poetry have gone in and out of popularity in British literary history. In this guide, you will study several early types of poems: *Beowulf* is an Old English heroic epic; *Sir Gawain and the Green Knight* is a medieval romance poem; *The Canterbury Tales* is a collection of Middle English narrative poems; finally, *Paradise Lost* is a seventeenth-century epic poem.

Drama

Drama is another ancient genre, one that is closely related to poetry, as early dramas were written largely in verse form. In the Western tradition, the principles and characteristics of drama have their roots in classical Greece. Although drama can be in prose or poetry, it has several distinct features.

Drama is written to be performed by actors in front of a collective audience, although it can be read as literature. For this reason, drama has limited description and focuses on dialogue and action. Some dramas are written word for word, while others have limited scripting and allow the actors to improvise. Types of dramas include comedy, tragedy, history, romance, and satire.

Famous British dramatists include Marlowe, Shakespeare, Shaw, and many others. This collection does not include specific works of drama, but the features of drama have influenced modern stage and film adaptations of most of the works you will read.

Prose

Prose fiction writing, in its commonly recognized forms (the novel, the short story), is one of the newest types of literature. Prose also includes nonfiction genres like biography and autobiography, as well as some dramas, but in this collection, you will read mostly novels and a few short stories. You will also read one biography, *Something Beautiful for God*.

The novel

A novel is recognizable as a lengthy work of prose fiction with a unified theme or story-line rather than a series of episodes, traditionally presenting realistic people and events. Because of its greater length, a novel may have multiple subplots and a variety of characters. Generally the **plot** is complex and may have twists or unexpected revelations. Modern novels are divided into chapters or sections.

Robinson Crusoe is sometimes considered the first true English novel. In addition to this early example of a novel, this guide will introduce you to a wide range of novels and novel derivatives, from social critiques to allegories, romances to children's novels.

The short story

In the nineteenth century, American writer Edgar Allan Poe was one of the first to define the short story form. He said a short story should be readable in one sitting and should produce a singular effect on the reader—usually a sense of horror, relief, or fear.

Not all short stories follow this model. However, the word "short," a loose term encompassing works from one paragraph to thirty or more pages in length, does have an effect on the scope of the genre. The plot must be relatively compact. Short stories often deal with a single, formative event in a character's life. Short stories are often limited to one **protagonist**. The focus of the story may be on the character's development, or the character may be a pawn in a sequence of larger events.

The short stories by Chesterton you will study in this collection are part of a specific category known as crime or detective stories.

UNDERSTANDING LITERATURE:
Devices and Conventions

Every writer is different. Each author approaches his or her subject from a different angle. Some writers have a specific purpose in writing: a moral or lesson they want the reader to learn. Others write out of a love of words and wordplay. Sometimes the writer focuses on unusual or complex characters. The writer's main interest may be a historical setting or problem.

At the same time as you enjoy the overall effect of a book, take time to notice the techniques the writer uses to get his or her point across. You may be wondering why this is important. Think of it in terms of traveling.

If you fall asleep while you are riding with someone in the car, you may arrive at a destination without knowing how you got there. That may be fine if you are traveling with people who are going to the same place you are. If, however, you are on a train or bus, you may miss your stop and end up somewhere you don't want to be, with no idea how you got there or where you went wrong.

The same idea applies when you read a book. You probably do not know the author personally, and you will not always read books by people who share your beliefs or worldview. The author may want to convince you to believe a certain way, or the book may contain assumptions you don't share. If you don't notice where the book is taking you, you may reach conclusions you disagree with, but you may not know at what point you headed down that path. For this reason, it is important to "stay awake" while you read.

By learning more about styles and techniques of writing, you will be better equipped to evaluate the book's messages and decide whether or not to accept the worldview and philosophy it contains.

As you read each book, take into account the length of chapters, the genre of the book, and the overall style and sentence structure. Consider the effectiveness of the author's writing style in light of your response to the book. Always keep in mind that the book was composed by a person who wrote with a particular style and probably had a reason for writing that way.

This section introduces some of the devices and conventions used in a work of literature. The unique style of an author is largely determined by these elements, and these are the subtle tools a writer uses (in addition to characters, setting, and plot) to get a point across.

Content

Content is one of the first things you should notice. What type of writing does the author use the most? Most works contain some combination of description, exposition, and dialogue. Description refers to passages that give visual information about the setting or the characters. Exposition is when the narrator tells you what happens. It includes action, commentary, or the passage of time. Dialogue refers to the characters' speech and is usually indicated by quotation marks. Dialogue may also be internal, when a character speaks to himself or herself.

Some books use one type of content almost exclusively. Others contain an even balance of all three. Do you notice when an author switches from exposition to description? What is the effect of using dialogue rather than exposition to show events? Why does an author give you so much description of one character and so little for another? Think about what effect each type of writing produces.

Language

The tone and language of a work of literature can be familiar and colloquial, using slang and phonetic spelling to show accents (Mark Twain's writing is a good example). It can be formal, scholarly, or even jumbled and confused. As you read, ask yourself questions about the author's use of language. Does the author use big words to describe scenes? Are there a lot of ambiguous or vague words?

Books are written deliberately, and characters are presented to create a definite impression. In general, every detail that is given about a character has some significance. Do the characters seem well-educated? Do all of them seem equally credible? If not, why not? If the characters philosophize or present a moral principle, do you take them seriously? Be aware of the way a character is described, what his or her physical and emotional traits are, and how he or she speaks.

Just as movies encourage you to cheer for a particular character, books also present some characters as more sympathetic than others. Language and voice have a lot to do with the way you, the reader, perceive the characters, the setting, and the message of each work.

Tense

Although most books are written in the past tense ("It was a dark and stormy night," "Once upon a time there was a princess"), the author chooses which dominant verb tense to use. Even within one tense, the author can use subtle changes to indicate continuous problems, distant versus recent past, and uncertainty. Each tense tells you something a little bit different.

Past tense can give you a sense of expectation or of building tension leading up to some great discovery or revelation. For example, *Jane Eyre* is told in the past tense. In that case, the narrator (Jane) is giving you background information that leads up to her present situation. Present tense might give you a greater sense of immediacy and involvement in the book. It would also give you less certainty about what is going to happen.

A book written in past tense tells you there is a definite ending. You know that the narrator, at least, has seen the end of the story. A book in present tense could stop unfinished or change narrators abruptly if something happens to the original one. When you read, take note of the main verb tense and ways verb tense influences the way you think about the narrator and about the outcome of the plot.

Perspective/Narrator

Some books have a clearly defined narrator. You know who is telling the story, what his or her role is in the story, and what he or she knows. Sometimes, however, the scenario is not as clear. The voice of the narrator may be distant and impersonal, or it may address the reader directly. Remember, even if the narrator is generic and impersonal, a narrator still exists. Someone is telling the story, and it is frequently someone other than the author.

The most basic concept of narration is "person." **First person** narration uses "I" and "we" to tell the story. For example, "I saw two hundred pirates approaching the beach." First person tells you that the narrator is experiencing or relating these events firsthand. If you see a first person narrator, ask yourself what the narrator reveals about himself or herself, and what his or her role is in the story.

Second person narration uses "you" to tell the story. For example, "You see two hundred pirates rushing toward you." Second person places you, the reader, in the story. Second person narration is very rare (one example is the young adult series *Choose Your Own Adventure*). Occasionally, however, a first or third person narrator will break into second person to address the reader directly. This strategy can be used to draw the reader into the plot, make a side comment, point out something the characters do not notice, or ask the reader to consider something personally.

The most common narration is **third person**, which uses "he," "she," "it," and "they." Third person removes both the reader and the narrator from the story and makes them outside observers rather than participants. Third person narration can be from the perspective of one of the characters, showing only what that character sees and going where he or she goes. It can also be impartial and jump from character to character.

The perspective may be **omniscient** (all-knowing) or **limited**. If the perspective is limited, the narrator knows only what one character knows. If the narration is from the perspective of a particular character, only that character's thoughts are written down. If the perspective is omniscient, the narrator can see everything that is happening, including things the characters cannot see or know. An omniscient narrator may also have access to the thoughts of multiple characters.

A **limited perspective** can lend a greater sense of mystery, while an omniscient perspective can create a sense of impending doom by showing the reader something the characters should see but cannot. An omniscient narrator can also create **irony** by revealing contradictions.

Remember, sometimes a book will combine several different types of perspective and narration. When you see the perspective change, ask yourself why it is changing, and what effect the new style has on the story's content.

Mood/Tone

The author creates mood or tone primarily through description and language. The setting also plays a significant role. Ask yourself how settings are described, including lighting, weather, cleanliness, and age or state of repair. Does everything take place in a darkened, ramshackle mansion? Does it rain a lot? Is nature portrayed as threatening, neutral, or pleasant? You will need to decide if descriptions are an attempt to portray a real setting accurately, or if they are symbolic.

Characters contribute to the mood or tone of a piece. Some characters are optimistic; others are pessimistic. If bad things always happen to the cheerful characters, how likely is it that the story will have a happy ending? At the end, are you left with a sense of hope? If so, why? The author can create mood by selecting the order of events, the characters' reactions to events, and the introductory or concluding scenes of the chapter or the book.

Finally, word choice also influences mood. A house may be shadowy and dark, or it may be gloomy and ominous. One description is relatively neutral; the other has negative connotations. In the same way, "happy" and "gleeful" might describe the same emotion, but they create very different tones. One style of writing that uses word choice to produce a certain effect is **satire**. By treating serious issues in a flippant manner or silly issues seriously, satires use humor to make a point.

Purpose

From all of these conventions and devices, you can begin to estimate the underlying purpose and worldview of the book. The possibilities are endless. The purpose of the book could be profit, moral training, social change, historical documentation, aesthetics (the pursuit of beauty), or personal fulfillment. The author could be proposing a different worldview, promoting social reform, working through an event in his or her past, or correcting a historical inaccuracy.

Keep in mind that this process is largely guesswork. Unless you have spoken to the author personally, you cannot know what he or she intended, and sometimes an author may be unaware of the attitudes and ideas the book reveals. However, you can evaluate the content and effects of the book and speculate about the author's intent. This exercise is also a good reminder that worldview has a tendency to show up in what you produce, with or without a conscious decision to put it in.

Writing Refinement

Sometimes it is easy to confuse good writing with vague writing or with using a lot of big words, but it is possible to write with refinement without sounding like a dictionary. There are a variety of ways to enhance your skills as a writer. (One of the best ways is to spend a lot of time reading because you will be able to see what is effective and what is not.) This collection introduces you to a few technical and analytic skills that will help you get started.

Three keys to good writing are clarity, precision, and sophistication. Clarity means you avoid using more words than you need to make your point. You say what you mean instead of rambling. Precision means you say exactly what you mean, nothing more and nothing less. You choose the best possible word to represent your intended meaning. Sophistication means you have a wide vocabulary, and you use varied sentence structure and transitions. You explain and use examples, you use appropriate terminology correctly, and you integrate quotations smoothly.

Practicing Clarity, Precision, and Sophistication

Sometimes native English speakers learn to write by instinct ("it sounds right!") rather than by a solid knowledge of English grammar. As you work to become a clearer, more sophisticated writer, it is a great time to go back and review the basics. One trait that distinguishes good writers from competent ones is the ability to use different types of sentences. Before you can do that, you will need to understand how sentences work. This section is not a thorough guide to English grammar, but it will help you identify some of the core concepts related to sentence structure. If one of the concepts or terms in this section is not clear to you, consider stopping to consult a grammar book before you continue.

There are four types of sentences: simple, compound, complex, and compound-complex.

> A **simple sentence** has one <u>independent clause</u>. An independent clause can stand by itself; it has a subject and a verb and does not rely on another clause to make a complete thought.
>
> Example: *The book was short.*

> A **compound sentence** has two or more independent clauses linked together by a semicolon or a coordinating conjunction like "and," "so," or "but."
>
> Example: *The book was short, so I read it quickly.*

> A **complex sentence** has one independent clause and at least one <u>dependent clause</u>. A dependent clause, as the name suggests, is not complete on its own. It has a subject and verb, but it is linked to another clause by a subordinating conjunction like "when," "because," or "if."
>
> Example: *The book was short because it was a children's book.*

> A **compound-complex** sentence has at least two independent clauses and at least one dependent clause.
>
> Example: *The book was short because it was a children's book, so I read it quickly.*

Every clause within a sentence follows one of seven possible sentence patterns:

S-V*i* (subject + intransitive verb)
    Example: *The boy ran.*

S-V*t*-DO (subject + transitive verb + direct object)
    Example: *The hero killed the dragon.*

S-V*l*-PN (subject + linking verb + predicate nominative)
    Example: *The writer was Charles Dickens.*

S-V*l*-PA (subject + linking verb + predicate adjective)
    Example: *The character is honest.*

S-V*t*-IO-DO (subject + transitive verb + indirect object + direct object)
    Example: *The stranger gave her an apple.*

S-V*t*-DO-OCN (subject + transitive verb + direct object + object complement noun)
    Example: *The good fairy made the servant a princess.*

S-V*t*-DO-OCA (subject + transitive verb + direct object + object complement adjective)
    Example: *The attention made him proud.*

When you read, stop periodically and test your ability to identify different types of sentences. As you write, make it your goal to use different sentence structures. Remember, it is great to be able to write "naturally," without thinking about grammar rules; however, if you ever want to teach someone else how to write, explain why a sentence is or is not grammatically correct, or accurately edit your own writing, it is important to understand the mechanics of writing as well.

Citing Sources

When you cite (quote or paraphrase) a work of literature in an essay, it is important, as with any other source, to give proper attribution. Writers and researchers put a lot of time into their work, and they deserve recognition for that effort. In academics, failure to give proper credit is called plagiarism. Plagiarism includes copying and pasting information from the Internet, paraphrasing or directly quoting someone else's words without giving them credit, and claiming someone else's ideas as your own.

There are several ways to use research correctly. You can use an author's words exactly, but you must use quotation marks. You can also paraphrase the author's words. Paraphrasing does not mean simply changing a word or two; it means completely rewriting the information in your own words **and** sentence structure. Whether you paraphrase or quote, you must include citations.

For writing about literature, the most common style for citations is from the Modern Language Association (MLA). MLA style uses a Works Cited page at the end of the paper, which contains full bibliographical information for each book, and parenthetical citations within the body of the paper, which give the author's last name—or title, if the author is unknown—and the page number of the quoted or paraphrased material.[2]

---

[2]*MLA Handbook* (see www.mla.org) is the best source for detailed information about this citation style.

The Works Cited entries are alphabetized by the author's last name, and each entry gives the author's name, the title of the work, the location of the publishing company, the publisher's name, and the date of publication (found on the copyright page of most books). When you cite a complete, stand-alone work, like a novel or play, the title should be in italics. If you cite part of a larger collection, like a story or poem, the title of the story should be in quotation marks, and it should be followed by the title of the collection in italics.

If you choose not to paraphrase, and instead you use the same words and sentence structure as the original, you need to put the information in quotation marks. If you take out part of a quote to save space or because it's not relevant to your argument, you should use an ellipsis […] to notify readers that you have modified the original and to indicate where material is missing.

In addition to these general guidelines for citations, quoting literature brings up a few unique concerns. Sometimes a quote from literature will include dialogue. Use single quotation marks ' ' for the dialogue within the quote and normal quotation marks " " for the outside of the quotation.

See the following example for a demonstration of correct citations:

In the text: "'They are indeed,' said Professor Godbole. 'Such affability is seldom seen.'" (Forster 67).

Works Cited entry: Forster, E.M. *A Passage to India*. Pleasantville, NY: Reader's Digest, 1989.

If you quote a poem, formatting the poem as it appears on the page takes up a lot of room. Instead, unless you are quoting more than four lines, use a backslash (/) to indicate line breaks. Because the whole poem may be on the same page, whenever possible your parenthetical citation should give the line numbers for your quote. If you cite the same poem multiple times, uses "lines" in the parenthetical the first time, and then shorten it to "ll." See the following example:

"So The Spear-Danes in days gone by / and the kings who ruled them had courage and greatness" (*Beowulf* lines 1-2).

Remember, although these particular rules are arbitrary and apply mainly to academic writing, tailoring your writing to a specified format is the same skill needed to write memos and reports, letters of application, resumes, grant proposals, newspaper articles, and many other writing tasks.

Analyzing Influences

There is more to writing than having good grammar and style (the mechanics of writing), although those are certainly important. Content—what you write—is even more important. As you become comfortable reading classic literature, you should begin to focus on ideas. Try not to treat all essays as book reports; instead, think of writing as starting a conversation with the author and the text. To do that, you have to read with depth and breadth.

Reading with depth means asking, what assumptions does this book make? How does it convey ideas? How is it structured? What devices does the author use, and to what effect?

Reading with breadth means asking, how does this book relate to other books? What outside influences and ideas does it reflect? Literature is not written in a vacuum. What that means is that literature is never completely free of the conditions in which it was created. Authors and their texts can interact with society in several ways: a work of literature can support social conventions either implicitly or explicitly; it can critique social conventions; it can also reject those conventions and attempt to establish its own. (This last category often appears in works of science fiction or fantasy.)

Looking at the social and cultural influences on a literary work sometimes requires background research. It is highly unlikely that you know the precise social conditions, for example, when *The Canterbury Tales* was written. However, if you go to the library or the Internet, you can find plenty of information about class identity and the reworking of social divisions in fourteenth-century England.

You might be surprised by the portrayal of slavery as natural in *Robinson Crusoe*, but after researching the history of slavery, you might find that it did not become illegal in England until 1772, years after Defoe's novel was published. While social customs may not excuse the treatment of slaves portrayed in literature, it can help to explain it.

After all, literature cannot help mirroring some of what is normal in society. As a conscientious reader, it is always wise to be aware of the conditions in which a piece of literature was written. Great literature can apply to modern situations, but each work was written in a specific context. As a sophisticated writer, you should take into account themes and ideas that were influential to the author.

Comparing Ideas

Not only do books relate to historical and social movements, but they also respond to other works of literature. Think about your own culture. What movies have produced sequels, spin-offs, and parodies? What characters and settings have name recognition even among people who haven't read the book or seen the movie?

Now apply those questions to classic literature. Some novels are written as a modern retelling or a critical rewrite of another book. Others quote or reference an earlier work. Sometimes two books approach the same issue from opposite directions, and sometimes they approach different issues from the same perspective.

For example, two books set during World War II might have very different perspectives if they were written by a German author and a British author. Sometimes a different genre shapes two books that would otherwise be very similar. You can learn a lot by finding the links—and distinctions—between two works of literature.

In addition, comparison is a prime opportunity to dissect an author's style. If two authors take on the same core idea, they will not produce the same work because each one has a unique writing style.

Finally, by comparing and contrasting two different works on the same subject, you can gain valuable insight into the way information can be interpreted differently based on your philosophy and worldview. Whether you like it or not, assumptions influence conclusions. Even in literature, authors' perspectives tend to give a particular slant to each topic they put on paper.

Applying Critical Lenses

Looking at the world "through rose-colored glasses" is a common way of saying someone always sees things as better than they really are. The phrase has a figurative meaning, but it is based on a real phenomenon: wearing a pair of tinted sunglasses can make you see the world differently as the distinction between certain colors fades or vanishes entirely. In the same way, when you read a novel, the "lens" through which you read has a real impact on what you see in the book.

Part of your "lens" as a reader is involuntary—based on your worldview, your experiences, and your preconceptions—and part of it is a choice of what interests you. Think about being in a book club or discussing a book with a friend. Some people are passionate about defending the actions of their favorite character. Others are interested in the way a book fits into its historical context, or in the details the author leaves out or brushes over.

People who study or teach literature do the same thing: they choose to focus on specific features of literature when they read based on what they find interesting or compelling. If you take a literature course in college or join a literature discussion group, you may be asked to think about the "lens" through which you read. First and foremost, identifying your own "lens" will make you a stronger, more conscientious reader. In addition, studying the lenses other literary critics have used will give you insight into the perspectives you may encounter in a conversation about literature.

As with any new vocabulary, you may find that you have been using the concepts already without knowing it. Remember, there is no master list of critical approaches, and new methods are developed all the time. The following three—Marxist, feminist/multicultural, and historicist—will give you a sample to get you started.

Marxist criticism pays attention to the underlying class struggle in a work of literature. Marx thought that art and literature reflect the society in which they were created, especially economic attitudes. Marxist criticism focuses on the portrayal of different economic classes. Does the book support the dominance of the middle and upper classes, or are you encouraged to sympathize with the lower, working classes? Does the book imply that social hierarchies are logical and natural, or does it point out their problems and contradictions?

Feminist and multicultural criticisms pay attention to the experiences of people groups in a work of literature (whether divided by race, gender, nation, or ethnicity). They focus on the way these groups are portrayed and how much or little power they have. Feminist criticism looks at the way the roles of women are reinforced or challenged by works of literature. Multicultural criticism emphasizes the way other cultural groups are empowered or minimized.

Historicist criticism pays attention to the history surrounding the creation of literature. It treats the literary work as a historical artifact and focuses on events that may have influenced the author's concerns or perspectives. Historicism looks at the circumstances at the time the book was written and draws parallels between the history and the resulting literature.

One, all, or none of these methods may match your interests, but even if you disagree with all of these approaches, being aware of the vocabulary of literary criticism will give you new ways to talk about literature with all different kinds of people, from scholars to coworkers, family, and friends.

Although these are secular categories of analysis, the underlying ideas of each of them can be compatible with a Christian worldview. The breakdown of relationships between rich and poor, advantaged and disadvantaged, and men and women is a clear sign of this world's imperfections. Analyzing different cultures in literature can reveal the diversity and beauty of creation and the people in it. Finally, history and literature are different types of expression, but each of them shows an important piece of the greater story of failure and redemption.

Using the Vocabulary

Every field has its own vocabulary. Much of the vocabulary of literary analysis is derived from everyday terms. Some words, however, have a different meaning when they are used in the context of literature. If you practice using the following words when you discuss literature, you will not only improve your vocabulary, but you will become a more precise, sophisticated writer in the process.

A word of caution: using big words does not make you a good writer, especially if you use them incorrectly. Special terminology is valuable when it is used sparsely, correctly, and only as needed.

These terms appear in **bold** in the rest of this book. Here, each word is defined and used in a sentence. If it is a literary technique, 1) the word is defined, 2) an example is given, and 3) the term is used in a sentence, as it might be in an essay about literature.

Literary Analysis Glossary

Allegory — A story with two levels of meaning, one that is literal, and one in which the characters, places, and events stand for something outside the story.

The Pilgrim's Progress is an allegory for the struggles a Christian undergoes on his or her journey through life.

Alliteration – When several words in a line use the same initial consonant sound or repeat the same vowel sound. This technique was used instead of or alongside rhyming in Old and Middle English poetry.

"The walls breached and burnt down to brands and ashes." From *Sir Gawain and the Green Knight*, Part 1. Here the sound "b" is emphasized repeatedly.

Sir Gawain and the Green Knight uses alliteration to emphasize key words in the poem.

Allusion – An indirect reference to another literary work or historical figure or event. Sometimes the reference is to a character; other times it refers to a famous line or quotation.

"Strong wind, earthquake-shock, and fire may pass by: but I shall follow the guiding of that still small voice which interprets the dictates of conscience." From Charlotte Brontë, *Jane Eyre*, chapter 19.

In this passage, Jane alludes to the "still small voice" mentioned in 1 Kings 19:11-12.

Antagonist – A character who opposes the hero of the story. Often, the antagonist shows the hero's character by contrast.

In *The Screwtape Letters*, traditional literary roles are switched because Screwtape takes the role of the protagonist, and the Enemy (God) is the literary antagonist.

Blank verse – Poetry that has meter (a set number of accented syllables per line) but not rhyme.

"The mind is its own place, and in itself / Can make a Heav'n of Hell, a Hell of Heav'n." From Milton, *Paradise Lost*, Book 1.

Milton defended his use of blank verse, calling rhyme "the invention of a barbarous age."

Bob and wheel – One line of two (occasionally three) syllables followed by four short rhyming lines. This device appears at the conclusion of stanzas in later Middle English poetry.

"most fair. / Where war and wrack and wonder / By shifts have sojourned there, / And bliss by turns with blunder / In that land's lot had share." From *Sir Gawain and the Green Knight*, Part 1.

The bob and wheel with which each stanza of *Sir Gawain* concludes often summarizes or reflects on the contents of the rest of the stanza.

Caesura – A grammatical pause or physical break in a line of poetry, which was used to divide the line in Old English and some Middle English poetry. A caesura (plural, caesurae or caesuras) is often symbolized by this mark: ||

"Sigemund's glory || grew and grew." From *Beowulf*, in a free-spoken poem told by a thane in King Hrothgar's court.

The poems told by members of the court in *Beowulf* are divided by caesurae, a common device in alliterative poems.

Climax – The height of tension or turning point in a story, when the book moves from building to resolving conflict.

In *The Hobbit*, the tensions between Bilbo, the dwarves, and the elves build until they reach a climax just before the Battle of Five Armies.

Conflict – Tensions or difficulties faced by the characters in a story. Conflict can be internal, like personal doubts, or external, like physical obstacles or enemies.

Charles Darnay's and Sydney Carton's mutual love for Lucie in *A Tale of Two Cities* is a consistent source of conflict between the two characters.

Epic poem — A long narrative poem about the life of a heroic figure, usually dealing with the struggle between good and evil and including other distinct features like a twelve-part structure, extensive battles, and lists of weapons and armor.

Milton composed *Paradise Lost* to tell the Christian story in the form of an epic poem.

First person – A grammatical structure in which the narrator uses the pronouns "I" or "we" to personally tell the story.

"Music and silence—how I detest them both!" From C.S. Lewis, *The Screwtape Letters*.

Because C.S. Lewis's Screwtape speaks to the reader in first person, the reader becomes privy to Screwtape's most personal thoughts about God and man.

Foreshadowing – An event that hints at something that will happen later.

> The dwarves' unwillingness to tell the Elvenking about the treasure, even if it means imprisonment, foreshadows the battle that will arise over ownership of the treasure.

Framework story – A story containing another story. Sometimes the inner story is told by a character in the frame story; sometimes the inner story is a play or story read or viewed by characters in the frame story.

> The framework story in *The Canterbury Tales* is a group of pilgrims telling each other stories as they ride along the road to Canterbury.

Free verse – Poetry that lacks regular meter and, often, rhyme as well.

> "Roses are planted where thorns grow, / And on the barren heath / Sing the honey bees." From William Blake, *The Marriage of Heaven and Hell*.

> Modern poetry is often written in free verse, so the poet is not tied down to specific forms.

Irony – An event, situation, action, or statement that reveals inconsistency, in which reality and appearance are different.

> An atheist cries "Oh God!" when a tornado strikes.

> It is ironic that Robinson Crusoe joins an expedition to buy slaves when he himself has recently escaped from slavery.

Kenning – A poetic name for a person, place, or thing, which consists of several descriptive words often joined by a hyphen. This technique was specifically used in Old English epic poetry.

> "So the guardian of the mound, / the hoard-watcher, waited for the gloaming." From *Beowulf*.

> In *Beowulf*, "Guardian of the mound" and "hoard-watcher" are kennings for the dragon.

Limited Perspective – When the narrator follows one character's perspective. Sometimes limited perspective also means the narrator cannot go inside the character's head or know his or her thoughts.

> *Pride and Prejudice* is told in limited perspective from Elizabeth Bennet's point of view.

Metaphor – An implicit comparison between two things, or between a character or event and a broader theme, concept, or idea.

> In *A Tale of Two Cities*, the women knitting under the guillotine are a metaphor for the French Revolutionary society, which existed under the perpetual shadow of death.

Meter – The rhythm of a poem, as conveyed by the number of (emphasized) syllables in a line. Meter consists of the type of "foot" or pattern of stresses, and the number of feet in a line.

> "I will not trouble thee, my child; farewell." From Shakespeare, *King Lear*, act 2, scene 4.

> Most of Shakespeare's plays are written in the same meter: iambic pentameter.

Narrator – The "voice" telling the story. Sometimes, but not always, the narrator is a character. The narrator can speak in first, second, or third person, and in past, present, or future tense.

The narrator of Forster's *A Passage to India* occasionally speaks to the reader in first person, indicating moments when the author wants to point out a broader social principle.

Omniscient Perspective – When the narrator is not limited to one character's point of view, but sees the larger picture. This term can also refer to a narrator who can see and know things that the characters do not, or who can see inside the characters' thoughts and emotions.

Because the narrator is omniscient in *A Tale of Two Cities*, readers see a bigger picture than the characters do.

Plot – The events or course of action that moves a story along.

Although the characters are complex, the basic plot of *Animal Farm* is relatively simple: a group of animals take over a farm, and their original communal spirit eventually disappears.

Point of view – The angle from which a story is told. Sometimes a narrator tells the story about characters, and sometimes a character tells his or her own story. Sometimes the story only follows what one character sees, and sometimes it jumps from character to character.

Because *Jane Eyre* is told from Jane's point of view, the reader does not know anything about the source of the mysterious laughter until Jane finds out.

Protagonist – The main character of a book, who is usually viewed in a positive light.

Since there are multiple main characters in Forster's novel, it is difficult to pinpoint the protagonist of *A Passage to India*.

Pun – A play on words that makes a subtle joke using words that sound the same but have different meanings.

"'Mine is a long and a sad tale!' said the Mouse, turning to Alice, and sighing. 'It is a long tail, certainly,' said Alice." From Lewis Carroll, *Alice in Wonderland*.

The characters in *Alice in Wonderland* repeatedly create puns on words like "tail" and "tale."

Rhyme – Two words that sound the same. In poetry, rhyme is often used to mark the end of a line.

"Whan that April with his showres soote / The droughte of March hath perced to the roote." From Chaucer, *The Canterbury Tales*, The General Prologue (Middle English version).

One of the difficulties of translating poetry is staying true to the original rhyme patterns.

Satire - A way of criticizing an idea or person by exaggerating their troubling characteristics to create humor, but with the ultimate goal of producing reform.

In "A Modest Proposal," Swift satirizes callous discussions of poverty by suggesting that poor children be killed to feed the rich.

Second Person – A grammatical structure using the pronoun "you," which places the reader within the story's action.

"You will find that a good many Christian-political writers think that Christianity began going wrong and departing from the doctrine of its Founder, at a very early stage." From C.S. Lewis, *The Screwtape Letters*, Letter 23.

Because C.S. Lewis's Screwtape addresses the reader in second person, the reader becomes another recipient of Screwtape's twisted advice to Wormwood.

Simile – An explicit comparison between two things, signified by the words "like," "as," or "than."

"All the same it was like trying to ride, without bridle or stirrups, a round-bellied pony that was always thinking of rolling on the grass." From J.R.R. Tolkien, *The Hobbit*.

Bilbo uses similes to describe his experience helping the dwarves escape the elves' palace.

Stanza – A segment of a poem, like a chapter in a book, composed of two or more lines. Stanzas generally have a consistent rhyme scheme or meter.

Each stanza of *Sir Gawain and the Green Knight* ends with a bob and wheel pattern.

Symbolism – The use of objects or characters to represent ideas.

It is symbolic that in the film version of *Pride and Prejudice*, Mrs. Bennet is often shown in between images of fluttering and squawking chickens.

Third Person – A grammatical structure, using the pronouns "he/she," "it," and "they" as subjects.

"The animals hated Moses because he told tales and did not work, but some of them believed in Sugarcandy Mountain." From George Orwell, *Animal Farm*.

Third person is the least involved "voice" and the most common in novels.

Beowulf
Author Unknown

Beowulf is one of very few surviving works from Anglo-Saxon, or Old English, literature. The author is unknown. The poem, which recounts the deeds of the hero Beowulf, is set in fifth or sixth century Scandinavia, but it was probably written in the eighth or ninth century in what is now England. The text was found in the *Cotton Vitellius A. xv* manuscript, also called the Nowell Codex after the earliest known owner. Although the original manuscript is housed in the British Library, several translations are available; one of the best was prepared by twentieth-century Irish poet Seamus Heaney.

UNDERSTANDING LITERATURE:
Genre

The heroic poem *Beowulf* is one of the first major works of literature in English. Nonetheless, you will read it in translation. Like any language, English has developed and changed over time. As a result, Old English is very different from the English spoken today, and modern readers would recognize few of the words.

Poems like *Beowulf* have much in common with oral narratives, stories that a bard or poet would recite to the nobility or to travelers along the road. The structure of *Beowulf*, like many Old English poems, is based on **alliteration** and **caesura** instead of **rhyme** and **meter**. In another technique common to Old English poetry, *Beowulf* uses multiple **kennings** to describe significant characters. Modern English translations may not re-create these characteristics precisely, but most keep the alliteration intact.

Beowulf is a heroic **epic poem**. Epic poetry, which has its roots in Greece, has many distinct characteristics. The following list gives some of the most recognizable. Keep in mind that not every epic poem includes all of these characteristics because the list was created after the poems in order to group and categorize them. In general, though, an epic poem:

Begins with the invocation of a muse or guiding spirit.

Begins in the middle of the action (*in medias res*).

Includes the statement of a theme.

Has a hero with superhuman qualities and almost godlike characteristics.

Lists and describes the hero's armor and weapons.

Contains extensive battle sequences.

Has a wide scope and usually covers the entire length of a hero's life.

Deals with the struggle between good and evil.

Has a 12-part structure.

As you read, think about which of these characteristics *Beowulf* fulfills. Which does it not fulfill? *Paradise Lost*, by John Milton, is also an epic, and *The Lord of the Rings*, by J.R.R. Tolkien, has been called a popular epic. If you have read these books, do you think they should be classified as epics? Why or why not?

Review Questions
1. Who were some of the good kings of the Spear-Danes?
2. What was done to Shield Sheafson's [Scyld-Scefing] body when he died?
3. What was the name of King Hrothgar's mead hall?
4. Who or what attacked the king's hall?
5. Who came to Hrothgar's aid?
6. With what weapons did Beowulf plan to fight Grendel?
7. How did Unferth challenge Beowulf at the feast? How did Beowulf respond?
8. Why could Beowulf's fellow warriors not injure Grendel?
9. How did Grendel die? What did he leave behind?
10. What did Hrothgar give Beowulf as tokens of his appreciation?
11. Who came to avenge Grendel?
12. Where did Grendel and his mother live?
13. Who gave Beowulf a sword to use against the monsters?
14. How did Beowulf kill Grendel's mother?
15. What advice did Hrothgar give Beowulf?
16. How did Beowulf gain the throne of the Geats? What disrupted the peace of his rule?
17. What had provoked the monster to anger?
18. Why did Beowulf choose to face the monster alone?
19. What was the result of Beowulf's battle with the monster?
20. What did Beowulf's comrades do during the battle?
21. Who stood by Beowulf?
22. What did Beowulf want to see before he died?
23. What did the Geats do with Beowulf's body?

Thought Questions
1. "Behavior that's admired is the path to power among people everywhere." Do you agree?
2. Grendel was described as a descendant of Cain. Why is this **allusion** significant?
3. When Beowulf arrived, his company was met by a warrior. If the warrior talked so courteously to armed strangers on his land, what does this tell you about the culture he represented?

4. Why do you think Beowulf felt obliged to help King Hrothgar defeat Grendel?
5. The men are called "a right people" because they were always ready to defend their lord. Is this same standard applicable today?
6. "It is always better to avenge dear ones than to indulge in mourning." Do you agree?
7. What kind of person is Unferth? What is his relationship to Beowulf?
8. Beowulf is said to have fought for "the glory of winning." Is this a noble reason? Discuss.
9. What made Beowulf a hero? Was he perfect? If not, why not?
10. What is the role of God in *Beowulf*?
11. If you have seen the 2007 movie version of *Beowulf*, what are some of the differences? Why do you think the writers, directors, and producers took those liberties?

WRITING REFINEMENT:
Practicing Clarity, Precision, and Sophistication

Keep in mind that there are many different ways to say the same thing. Rewriting sentences to use different structures and patterns will make you a stronger and more interesting writer. Take a look at the following example:

Example: Beowulf destroys the monster that is killing King Hrothgar's people.

Variation: When a monster attacks King Hrothgar's people, Beowulf answers the king's call for help.

Start by identifying the main kernel of the sentence (the subjects and verbs).

Example: Beowulf destroys ~~the monster that is killing King Hrothgar's people~~.

Variation: When ~~a~~ monster attacks ~~King Hrothgar's~~ people, Beowulf answers ~~the king's~~ call ~~for help~~.

Once you have eliminated the modifiers, you will see that the original sentence is a **simple sentence** (it has one independent clause), and it is an example of an **S-V*t*-DO** sentence pattern. The variation turns the sentence into a **complex sentence** (it has a dependent clause followed by an independent clause). The dependent and independent clauses are still in the **S-V*t*-DO** pattern.

Now it's your turn. For each of the following sentences, identify the sentence structure and the sentence pattern(s) of the original, and then rewrite each sentence using a different structure and/or pattern. Feel free to break the idea into two or more sentences to experiment with different lengths.

1. *Beowulf* is an Old English poem by an anonymous author about a Scandinavian hero.
2. *Beowulf* is an epic poem because, for example, it has a hero with superhuman qualities.
3. Beowulf defeats Grendel and his mother, but he is ultimately killed by the dragon.

Selections from

The Canterbury Tales

Geoffrey Chaucer

Geoffrey Chaucer (c.1343-1400) was born into the rising middle class in fourteenth-century England. During his lifetime, Chaucer held a variety of civil service roles. He worked as a diplomat for King Edward, and he was a customs official for a London port. Later in life, he was a justice of the peace and a Member of Parliament. Chaucer's occupations brought him into contact with people from all social classes. These experiences are reflected in his poetry. One of his most famous works is *The Canterbury Tales*, a collection of poetic tales written in the late 1300s.

UNDERSTANDING LITERATURE: *Devices and Conventions*

Language contributes to the mood of literature, but it also develops characters and gives them credibility—or takes it away. One character whom you may not always notice, but whose voice is also influenced by language, is the narrator.

Look at the following passages (in translation) describing the knight and the squire. Write down your impression of each character. Then look at the words used to describe that person. Underline the words that contributed to your impression. What do you learn about the narrator from these descriptions? Circle words that contribute to your impression of the narrator.

KNIGHT

> Of mortal battles he had fought fifteen,
> And he'd fought for our faith at Tramissene
> Three times in duels, always killed his foe.
> This self-same worthy knight had been also
> At one time with the lord of Palatye
> Against another heathen in Turkey:
> And always won he widespread fame for prize.

SQUIRE

Some twenty years of age he was, I guess.
In stature he was of average length,
Wondrously active, agile, and great of strength.
He'd ridden sometime with the cavalry
In Flanders, in Artois, and Picardy,
And conducted well within that little space
In hope to win thereby his lady's grace.

PROLOGUE

	Here bygynneth the Book of the Tales of Caunterbury	Here begins the Book of the Tales of Canterbury
1	Whan that aprill with his shoures soote	When April with his showers sweet with fruit
2	The droghte of march hath perced to the roote,	The drought of March has pierced unto the root,
3	And bathed every veyne in swich licour	And bathed each vein with liquor that has power
4	Of which vertu engendred is the flour;	To generate therein and sire the flower;
5	Whan zephirus eek with his sweete breeth	When Zephyr also has, with his sweet breath,
6	Inspired hath in every holt and heeth	Quickened again, in every holt and heath,
7	Tendre croppes, and the yonge sonne	The tender shoots and buds, and the young sun
8	Hath in the ram his halve cours yronne,	Into the Ram one half his course has run,
9	And smale foweles maken melodye,	And many little birds make melody
10	That slepen al the nyght with open ye	That sleep through all the night with open eye
11	(so priketh hem nature in hir corages);	(So Nature pricks them on to ramp and rage) —
12	Thanne longen folk to goon on pilgrimages,	Then do folk long to go on pilgrimage,
13	And palmeres for to seken straunge strondes,	And palmers to go seeking out strange strands,
14	To ferne halwes, kowthe in sondry londes;	To distant shrines well known in sundry lands.
15	And specially from every shires ende	And specially from every shire's end
16	Of engelond to caunterbury they wende,	Of England they to Canterbury wend,
17	The hooly blisful martir for to seke,	The holy blessed martyr there to seek
18	That hem hath holpen whan that they were seeke.	Who helped them when they lay so ill and sick.
19	Bifil that in that seson on a day,	Befell that, in that season, on a day
20	In southwerk at the tabard as I lay	In Southwark, at the Tabard, as I lay
21	Redy to wenden on my pilgrymage	Ready to start upon my pilgrimage
22	To caunterbury with ful devout corage,	To Canterbury, full of devout homage,
23	At nyght was come into that hostelrye	There came at nightfall to that hostelry
24	Wel nyne and twenty in a compaignye,	Some nine and twenty in a company
25	Of sondry folk, by aventure yfalle	Of sundry persons who had chanced to fall

26	In felaweshipe, and pilgrimes were they alle,	In fellowship, and pilgrims were they all
27	That toward caunterbury wolden ryde.	That toward Canterbury town would ride.
28	The chambres and the stables weren wyde,	The rooms and stables spacious were and wide,
29	And wel we weren esed atte beste.	And well we there were eased, and of the best.
30	And shortly, whan the sonne was to reste,	And briefly, when the sun had gone to rest,
31	So hadde I spoken with hem everichon	So had I spoken with them, every one,
32	That I was of hir felaweshipe anon,	That I was of their fellowship anon,
33	And made forward erly for to ryse,	And made agreement that we'd early rise
34	To take oure wey ther as I yow devyse.	To take the road, as you I will apprise.
35	But nathelees, whil I have tyme and space,	But none the less, whilst I have time and space,
36	Er that I ferther in this tale pace,	Before yet farther in this tale I pace,
37	Me thynketh it acordaunt to resoun	It seems to me accordant with reason
38	To telle yow al the condicioun	To inform you of the state of every one
39	Of ech of hem, so as it semed me,	Of all of these, as it appeared to me,
40	And whiche they weren, and of what degree,	And who they were, and what was their degree,
41	And eek in what array that they were inne;	And even how arrayed there at the inn;
42	And at a knyght than wol I first bigynne.	And with a knight thus will I first begin.

THE KNIGHT'S TALE

	The Knight's Portrait	The Knight
43	A knyght ther was, and that a worthy man,	A knight there was, and he a worthy man,
44	That fro the tyme that he first bigan	Who, from the moment that he first began
45	To riden out, he loved chivalrie,	To ride about the world, loved chivalry,
46	Trouthe and honour, fredom and curteisie.	Truth, honour, freedom and all courtesy.
47	Ful worthy was he in his lordes werre,	Full worthy was he in his leige-lord's war,
48	And therto hadde he riden, no man ferre,	And therein had he ridden (none more far)
49	As wel in cristendom as in hethenesse,	As well in Christendom as heathenesse,
50	And evere honoured for his worthynesse.	And honoured everywhere for worthiness.
51	At alisaundre he was whan it was wonne.	At Alexandria, he, when it was won;
52	Ful ofte tyme he hadde the bord bigonne	Full oft the table's roster he'd begun

53	Aboven alle nacions in pruce;	Above all nations' knights in Prussia.
54	In lettow hadde he reysed and in ruce,	In Latvia raided he, and Russia,
55	No cristen man so ofte of his degree.	No christened man so oft of his degree.
56	In gernade at the seege eek hadde he be	In far Granada at the siege was he
57	Of algezir, and riden in belmarye.	Of Algeciras, and in Belmarie.
58	At lyeys was he and at satalye,	At Ayas was he and at Satalye
59	Whan they were wonne; and in the grete see	When they were won; and on the Middle Sea
60	At many a noble armee hadde he be.	At many a noble meeting chanced to be.
61	At mortal batailles hadde he been fiftene,	Of mortal battles he had fought fifteen,
62	And foughten for oure feith at tramyssene	And he'd fought for our faith at Tramissene
63	In lystes thries, and ay slayn his foo.	Three times in lists, and each time slain his foe.
64	This ilke worthy knyght hadde been also	This self-same worthy knight had been also
65	Somtyme with the lord of palatye	At one time with the lord of Palatye
66	Agayn another hethen in turkye.	Against another heathen in Turkey:
67	And everemoore he hadde a sovereyn prys;	And always won he sovereign fame for prize.
68	And though that he were worthy, he was wys,	Though so illustrious, he was very wise
69	And of his port as meeke as is a mayde.	And bore himself as meekly as a maid.
70	He nevere yet no vileynye ne sayde	He never yet had any vileness said,
71	In al his lyf unto no maner wight.	In all his life, to whatsoever wight.
72	He was a verray, parfit gentil knyght.	He was a truly perfect, gentle knight.
73	But, for to tellen yow of his array,	But now, to tell you all of his array,
74	His hors were goode, but he was nat gay.	His steeds were good, but yet he was not gay.
75	Of fustian he wered a gypon	Of simple fustian wore he a jupon
76	Al bismotered with his habergeon,	Sadly discoloured by his habergeon;
77	For he was late ycome from his viage,	For he had lately come from his voyage
78	And wente for to doon his pilgrymage.	And now was going on this pilgrimage.

The General Prologue

Review Questions
1. When did people often set off on pilgrimages?
2. What was their destination?
3. How many were in the narrator's company?
4. Briefly describe the travelers (name, appearance, personality, or distinguishing characteristics).
   Knight
   Squire
   Yeoman
   Monk
   Prioress
   Friar
   Merchant
   Clerk
   Lawyer
   Franklin
   Haberdasher
   Carpenter
   Weaver
   Dyer
   Arras-maker
   Cook
   Sailor
   Physician
   Wife of Bath
   Parson
   Plowman
   Miller
   Manciple
   Reeve
   Summoner
   Pardoner
   Host

5. What did the narrator ask of his listeners after he listed the pilgrims?
6. What did the Host encourage the company to do along the way?
7. Who drew the shortest straw, indicating that he/she should tell the first tale?

Thought Questions
1. Why do you think Chaucer included the character details that he did?
2. The group was of many social classes. What would be a comparable group of people today?
3. What is the effect of telling stories within a story? Do you pay attention to all stories equally?
4. What is the relationship between the **framework story** and the stories within it?

The Knight's Tale

Review Questions

1. Who stopped Thesëus and his bridal party on the road?
2. Whom did Thesëus find among the dead of Thebes? What did he do with them?
3. Whom did Palamon see in the garden?
4. What caused Palamon and Arcita to quarrel?
5. How did Arcita get out of prison? On what condition was he released?
6. Under what guise did Arcita return to Athens? To what position was he promoted?
7. How did Palamon escape prison?
8. How/where did Palamon and Arcita meet? What did they agree to do?
9. Who revealed the fighters' identities to Thesëus?
10. Why did Thesëus pardon them? What did he decree?
11. What did Palamon ask from Venus on the day of the battle?
12. What did Emily (Emelye) ask from Diana? What was her answer?
13. What did Arcita ask from Mars?
14. What was the outcome of the tournament?
15. What happened to Arcita when he went to salute Emily?
16. What was Arcita's last request?
17. What did Thesëus tell Emily and Palamon to do?

Thought Questions

1. Is there a difference between "affection of holiness" and love?
2. Arcita makes the argument that love is the greatest law. Do you agree? Why or why not?
3. Would it be better to be in prison and be able to see your love or to be free and separated?
4. How do people today demonstrate their love? Are these ways as extreme, in your opinion?
5. Is it odd that the two men would help each other dress for battle against each other?
6. What does this tell you about the code of a knight?
7. Is it still considered noble to fight for a lady? Why or why not?
8. How would you describe Arcita's character? Palamon's? Emily's?
9. Why do you think Thesëus mourned for Arcita?
10. Is there a moral to this tale? If so, what is it?

WRITING REFINEMENT:
Using the Vocabulary

Chaucer's poetry is complex and intricately crafted. He used both rhyme and some alliteration to structure his poems. Look at the following passage from the General Prologue. The version on the left is in Middle English. Underline the words that rhyme (it may be tricky since Middle English pronunciation is different from modern English, but give it your best attempt). If there is any alliteration, underline that as well. The first two lines are done for you. Compare this version to a modern English version, included parallel to it.

Middle English	Modern English
Now have I told you smoothly in a <u>clause</u>	Now have I told you briefly, in a <u>clause</u>,
Th'estaat, th'array, the nombr e, and eek the <u>cause</u>	The state, the array, the number, and the <u>cause</u>
Why that assembled was this compaignye	Of the assembling of this company
In Southwerk at this gentil hostelrye	In Southwark, at this noble hostelry
That highte the Tabard, faste by the Belle,	Known as the Tabard Inn, closely to the Bell.
But now the time has come wherein to tell	But now is time to you for to tell
How that we baren us that ilke night	How we conducted ourselves that very night
Whan we were in that hostelrye alight.	When at the hostelry we did alight.
And after wol I tell of oure viage,	And afterward the story I begin
Al al the remenant of oure pilgrimage.	To tell you of our pilgrimage we're in.

Sir Gawain and the Green Knight
The *Pearl* Poet

Sir Gawain and the Green Knight is a Middle English poem from the late fourteenth century, written by an unknown British author. The poem was found with three other religious poems apparently by the same author, who has become known as the *Pearl* Poet after one of the other poems. The poem was found in the *Cotton Nero A.x.* manuscript, which is now housed in the British Library. Set in the Camelot of King Arthur and the Round Table, *Sir Gawain* is exemplary in its depiction of the chivalrous culture of the knight.

UNDERSTANDING LITERATURE:
Genre

Sir Gawain and the Green Knight is a medieval romance poem. Like many others, it deals with the court of the mythical King Arthur. Modern English versions are translations, and different translations may have slight discrepancies in the language that is used. The general form of the poem, however, remains consistent. The poem is divided into four books, each with twenty to thirty stanzas. At the end of each stanza is a distinctive poetic device called the **bob and wheel**: a very short line followed by four rhymed lines.

Look at the following **stanza**. Identify the bob and wheel and write one sentence describing why the wheel is important to the rest of the stanza. For practice, underline the **alliteration** and the words that rhyme (in the bob and wheel). The first two lines are done for you.

And since this <u>B</u>ritain was <u>b</u>uilt by this <u>b</u>aron great,

<u>B</u>old <u>b</u>oys <u>b</u>red there, in <u>b</u>roils delighting,

That did in their day many a deed most dire.

More marvels have happened in this merry land

Than in any other I know, since that olden time,

But of those that here built, of British kings,

King Arthur was counted most courteous of all,

Wherefore an adventure I aim to unfold,

That a marvel of might some men think it,

And one unmatched among Arthur's wonders.

If you will listen to my lay but a little while,

As I heard it in hall, I shall hasten to tell

anew.

As it was fashioned featly

In tale of derring-do,

And linked in measures meetly

By letters tried and true.

Book I (stanzas 1-21)

Review Questions
1. Which king of England was most honored?
2. What time of year did the story begin?
3. What interrupted the feasting?
4. What was unusual about the stranger? What two things did the stranger carry?
5. Why had he come? Who answered his challenge?
6. What was the result of Gawain's blow?
7. Where did the stranger live? What was his name?

Thought Questions
1. What is *chivalry*?
2. The knight sought Gawain's name as proof of fidelity. How do people judge credibility today?

Book II (stanzas 22-45)

Review Questions
1. When did Gawain depart on his quest?
2. What did the pentangle symbolize?
3. Where did Gawain arrive on Christmas Eve?
4. What did the lord tell Gawain about his quest?
5. What pact did Gawain make with the master of the house?

Thought Questions
1. Why do you think the number five was so important in medieval culture?
2. The characteristics important to a knight were generosity, friendliness, chastity, chivalry, and piety. Could this list also refer to the qualities of a good man? Of a Christian? Discuss.

Book III (stanzas 46-79)

Review Questions
1. What did the hunters pursue the first day?

2. Who visited Gawain in his bedroom? What did she ask him to do?
3. What did Gawain and the lord exchange at the end of the first day?
4. What did the hunters pursue the second day?
5. What did Gawain and the lord exchange at the end of the second day?
6. What did the hunters pursue the third day?
7. What did the lady give Gawain? How did she convince him to take her gift?
8. How did Gawain deceive the lord that night?

Thought Questions
1. Did medieval writers have a better understanding of romance than writers today? Explain.
2. Why do you think the author detailed the carving up of the hunters' game?
3. Is there anything significant about the three kinds of animals that the hunters pursued?

Book IV (stanzas 80-101)

Review Questions
1. What did Gawain's guide encourage him to do?
2. Why did the green knight withhold his first stroke?
3. What was significant about the blows the green knight gave Gawain?
4. Why did Gawain curse himself?
5. Why did he take the girdle with him when he left?
6. Who was the green knight? Where did he get his power?
7. Who was Morgan le Fay? How was she related to Gawain?
8. What gave distinction to the Round Table?

Thought Questions
1. How are cowardice and covetousness related?
2. Gawain attributed the fall of many great men to the temptation of women. Discuss. In the instances he named, were the women or the men at fault? Does it matter?
3. Gawain believed that a blemish on human conscience can be covered but not removed. Do you agree? Explain.

WRITING REFINEMENT:
Citing Sources

Integrating quotations into your writing is a vital part of analyzing literature. Any argument you make about a book or poem should be backed up by evidence from the text itself. Quoting poetry is a little more complicated than quoting prose. Although recommended methods may vary, the following guidelines will help you get started.

First, because replicating a poem as it appears on the page takes up a lot of space, use a backslash (/) instead to indicate the break between lines of a poem. Second, include the line numbers (when you can find them) instead of the page number in the parenthetical citation.

Look at the following lines of poetry from *Sir Gawain*. Integrate the quote into the paragraph below, formatting the citation properly. *Hint: when there is no author's name, use a shortened version of the title in your parenthetical citation.*

> "Your cut taught me cowardice, care for my life,
> And coveting came after, contrary both
> To largesse and loyalty belonging to knights."

From *Sir Gawain and the Green Knight*, lines 2379-2381.

Paragraph

In *Sir Gawain and the Green Knight*, Sir Gawain exemplifies the characteristics of a chivalrous knight. When he fails to uphold those characteristics by deceiving his host, he recognizes that he deserves the Green Knight's censure. He thanks the Green Knight for reminding him of his duty to uphold the standards of courtly behavior.

Paradise Lost, Book 1
John Milton

John Milton (1608-1674) was a seventeenth-century poet and political writer. During the English Civil War, he used his skills as a writer to advance the Parliamentary cause against Charles I and the Royalists. Much of Milton's writing, including *Paradise Lost*, was done by transcribers, as Milton became blind from glaucoma relatively early in his life. After Charles II was restored to the throne of England in 1660, Milton was imprisoned briefly for his political allegiances, but he continued to write. *Paradise Lost*, often considered his greatest work, was finally published in 1667.

UNDERSTANDING LITERATURE: *Genre*

Milton created *Paradise Lost* using the form of an epic poem. It was first published in ten parts, but the second edition, published just seven years later, was broken into twelve parts. As a reminder, here are some of the distinguishing characteristics of epic poetry. As you read, try to identify how Milton's poem fulfills each characteristic.

Begins with the invocation of a muse or guiding spirit.

Begins in the middle of the action (*in medias res*).

Includes the statement of a theme.

Has a hero with superhuman qualities and almost godlike characteristics.

Lists and describes a hero's armor and weapons.

Contains extensive battle sequences.

Has a wide scope and usually covers the entire length of a hero's life.

Deals with the struggle between good and evil.

Has a 12-part structure.

Paradise Lost is written in **blank verse**, using **alliteration**. Blank verse means that Milton's poem still has a regular **meter**, or number of accented syllables in each line, but it does not use **rhyme**. Look at the first five lines of the poem, reprinted below.

> Of man's first disobedience, and the fruit
> Of that forbidden tree, whose mortal taste
> Brought death into the world, and all our woe,
> With loss of Eden, till one greater man
> Restore us, and regain the blissful seat

How many syllables are in each line? How many are accented? A syllable is accented if it is emphasized when spoken. For example, you would say WHISpering rather than whisPERing or whisperING. (In this example, the first syllable is accented.)

Review Questions
  1. Whom did Milton invoke as his "muse"?
  2. To what cause did Milton attribute the fall of man?
  3. How did Milton describe the place where Satan was thrown from Heaven?
  4. Which fallen angel was named as next to Satan in power?
  5. By what names were the main fallen angels later known to man?
  6. What did Satan say should characterize the fallen angels' fight from that point on?
  7. What did the fallen angels build? Who was the architect? What was their new capital called?
  8. How did all of the fallen angels fit into the meeting place?

Thought Questions
  1. Why did God leave Satan free to execute his "dark designs"? Do you agree with Milton?
  2. "The mind is its own place, and in itself / Can make a Heav'n of Hell, a Hell of Heav'n." Discuss. Do you agree?
  3. What does "Better to reign in Hell than serve in Heav'n" mean? Have you ever felt this way?
  4. By what names would the fallen angels be called by humans today?
  5. Some critics, like the poet William Blake, have argued that Satan is the hero of Milton's poem. Do you think Milton romanticizes the character of Satan? Why or why not?
  6. What makes Satan a powerful orator? Do you think Milton presents an accurate picture of Satan's lies?

WRITING REFINEMENT: *Using the Vocabulary*

Having a good vocabulary enables you to write well. Reading a paper that uses the same words over and over again quickly becomes tedious. Look at the following sentences. Each one uses a few words repeatedly. Try to find substitute words that convey the same meaning but give the sentence variation. Keep in mind that it is not always best to choose a longer word; too many big words can make a paper sound awkward and stilted. Choose the most appropriate word rather than the most obscure.

1. Reading a poem like *Paradise Lost* is interesting because Satan is an interesting character, and Milton makes a familiar story more interesting.

2. *Paradise Lost* shows the story of Adam and Eve from a different perspective and gives the reader a different perspective on the story of the Garden of Eden.

3. Although some people picture Satan as an ugly creature, Milton pictures him as a beautiful creature because he was once an angel.

The Pilgrim's Progress
John Bunyan

John Bunyan (1628-1688) made a living as a tinker and a soldier until 1653, when he converted to Christianity. After his conversion, Bunyan became an outspoken preacher who was jailed for twelve years because he refused to stop preaching without a license. While imprisoned, Bunyan turned to writing and began his most famous work, *The Pilgrim's Progress*, which was published in two parts, the first in 1678, and the second in 1684.

UNDERSTANDING LITERATURE: *Genre*

The Pilgrim's Progress is an **allegory**—a story in which the characters, places, and events represent something else. Bunyan's book is easily identifiable as an allegory because he names his characters and locations according to their defining characteristics. Readers do not expect a character named Faithful to be faithless, and they are prepared to find pride and excess in a place called Vanity Fair.

Not all of Bunyan's names are this straightforward, however. Look at the following list of characters and places and write down a few characteristics you would expect them to have based on their names. As you read, look back at your list and see if you interpreted the names correctly.

Mr. Worldly Wiseman

Simple

Formalist

Adam the First

Mr. Talkative

By-ends

Watchful

Mt. Sinai

Valley of the Shadow of Death

Plain Ease

Review Questions
1. Why was the man in the dream in anguish?
2. What did Evangelist tell the man to do?
3. Who accompanied Christian toward the gate? Why did he turn back?
4. What advice did Worldly Wiseman give Christian? What prevented Christian from taking it?
5. What did the Interpreter show Christian?
6. When and how did Christian lose his burden?
7. Why did Christian turn back at the top of the Hill of Difficulty?
8. What was Christian shown at the Palace Beautiful?
9. How did Christian defeat Apollyon?
10. Who became Christian's companion?
11. What was Talkative's greatest fault?
12. Describe Vanity Fair. How did the occupants of the fair treat pilgrims?
13. What happened to Faithful?
14. Who left the fair with Christian?
15. Where and why did Christian leave the Way?
16. How did Christian and Hopeful escape Giant Despair?
17. What enabled the pilgrims to see the Gates of the Celestial City?
18. What two precautions did Christian propose against the possibility of robberies?
19. Of what did the man with the whip convict Christian and Hopeful?
20. What was the last difficulty before the City?
21. Why was Ignorance unable to enter at the Gate?

Thought Questions
1. Why does conviction of sin often result in despair? What is the remedy for this despair?
2. Why is legality not a substitute for grace?
3. What do you think the chained lions outside the Palace Beautiful represented?
4. Are parents responsible for the salvation of their children? Discuss.
5. Why do you think God allows his people to suffer and be tempted?
6. Why were the two giants in the Valley of the Shadow of Death named Pope and Pagan? Why did Bunyan say these two pitfalls were impotent?
7. Is there a common theme in the trials Christian faced? Those that Faithful faced? Explain.
8. How are Christianity, humility, and ambition related?
9. What is the difference between crying out against sin and abhorring sin?
10. "It is easier going out of the way when we are in, than going in when we are out." Why?
11. How does faith keep the flesh from holding sway?

12. Christian said it is wiser to avoid spiritual enemies than to confront them. Do you agree?

13. Why did Christian struggle more with death than Hopeful did?

14. Who had the stronger faith, Christian or Hopeful? Why? Does it matter?

15. Is it possible to "meet with joy" in Heaven every Christian you have ever known? Discuss.

WRITING REFINEMENT:
Practicing Clarity, Precision, and Sophistication

Clarity should always be one of your first priorities when you think about sentence structure. Below are several extremely long sentences. They are grammatically correct, but they are so long that the message becomes lost. Try to break them into several smaller sentences, or see if you can figure out another way to simplify them. For additional practice, identify the main elements in these sentences and try to identify what type of structure and patterns are being used in each example.

1. In John Bunyan's *The Pilgrim's Progress*, Christian, a new believer, makes his way from the City of Destruction to the Celestial City, helped along the way by other believers; he is also tested and tempted by people who are not true believers or who are outright enemies of God.

2. Vanity Fair is a place in John Bunyan's *The Pilgrim's Progress* where a new believer, Christian, has to face the scorn and anger of people who are in opposition to Christianity and who want to prevent Christian and his friend Faithful from continuing on their journey.

3. In order for Christian finally to reach the Celestial City in Bunyan's *The Pilgrim's Progress*, he has to rely on the help of other believers and messengers of God because he is not strong enough to resist the temptations and dangers of the enemy on his own and would lose his way if he was on his own.

Gulliver's Travels
Jonathan Swift

Jonathan Swift (1667-1745) was a noted Irish satirist. Originally a priest in the Church of Ireland, Swift became involved in the political struggles of the Whigs and Tories, political parties in England at the beginning of the eighteenth century. After the rise of King George I, Swift returned to Ireland, where he championed Irish political causes and wrote notable satires like "A Modest Proposal," which sarcastically advocated killing impoverished children in order to feed the rich. *Gulliver's Travels*, a book-length satire, was published in Ireland in 1726.

UNDERSTANDING LITERATURE:
Devices and Conventions

Writing tracts and pamphlets that ridicule a particular system can be an effective means of protest. However, those who disagree with the author will probably not read the pamphlets, and, if they do, they will reject the contents before they even begin to read. This is one reason **satire** is so effective. Satire takes an accepted idea and blows it out of proportion until it seems utterly ridiculous. The goal is to demonstrate that ideas which are preposterous on a large scale may also be problematic on a small scale. Swift was a master of this technique.

Look at the following statements. Think of a way you could broaden their scope to make them impractical or foolish. For this exercise, you do not have to agree with the satirical point you are making. Also keep in mind that things which are invalid when applied broadly are not necessarily invalid when applied locally. Satire is meant to obscure details, and it may not always reflect social conditions or historical figures accurately. The first one is an example.

Americans should honor the American flag. < The American flag should be worshipped.

Children should spend more time reading. <

Drivers should carpool to save gas. <

Individuals should take precautions to avoid getting sick. <

Part 1: A Voyage to Lilliput

Review Questions
1. Why did Gulliver go to sea? How did he become separated from his companions?
2. What happened while Gulliver slept? Who was responsible? How did Gulliver punish them?
3. What did the emperor decide to do with Gulliver?
4. What was the goal of the rope dancers? How did the Emperor reward his ministers' agility?
5. Under what conditions was Gulliver set free?
6. What two evils confronted Lilliput?
7. Why were Lilliput and Blefuscu at war?
8. Why did Reldresal tell Gulliver the affairs of state?
9. How did Gulliver capture the Blefuscan fleet? How did he defeat the enemy archers?
10. Why did Gulliver lose the favor of the emperor?
11. Why were the dead buried with their hands directly downward?
12. What were the differences between public nurseries for males and for females?
13. Why did Gulliver lose credit with the Emperor?
14. Of what was Gulliver accused? What sentence did Reldresal propose?
15. How did Gulliver respond to Reldresal's threat?
16. What did Gulliver see off the coast?
17. Why did Gulliver leave Blefuscu in haste?
18. How was Gulliver rescued? How did he prove he was telling the truth?

Thought Questions
1. Why was Gulliver bound by the laws of hospitality after he received gifts?
2. Do you think politicians ever get elected based on their ability to entertain? Discuss.
3. What is Swift satirizing by the Lilliputians' unusual means of swearing oaths?
4. Have you ever "conjectured" another explanation because you did not like the truth?
5. Why do you think nations go to war? Is it because of big causes or trivial events?
6. "Of so little weight are the greatest services to princes, when put into the balance with a refusal to gratify their passions." Discuss. Do you agree?
7. What did Swift think about courts and ministers, based on this book?
8. Do you think fraud or theft is a worse crime? Why?
9. Is it more effective to enforce laws with rewards, punishments, or both? Why?
10. Are most people chosen for jobs based on their moral standards or their abilities? Discuss.

Part 2: A Voyage to Brobdingnag

Review Questions

1. Why was Gulliver stranded on the island?
2. What was unusual about the island of Brobdingnag?
3. How was Gulliver discovered? What was the reaction of the inhabitants?
4. Who was Gulliver's teacher and companion?
5. Why was the old neighbor problematic for Gulliver?
6. How did Gulliver earn money for his master?
7. To whom was Gulliver sold, and why?
8. What did the king's scholars conclude about Gulliver?
9. Why did the dwarf not get along with Gulliver?
10. How did Gulliver travel?
11. Why did Glumdalclitch become afraid to let Gulliver out of her sight?
12. What was Gulliver's greatest danger in Brobdingnag?
13. How did Gulliver entertain the king and queen?
14. Why did the king want to hear about England? How did he sum up what Gulliver said?
15. What knowledge did Gulliver offer the king? How did the king respond?
16. What was the army made of?
17. How did Gulliver acquire his freedom?

Thought Questions

1. How are greatness and littleness determined? Is everything based on comparisons?
2. Why is it ignoble to be shown off because you are different?
3. The prince remarked on the contemptible nature of human grandeur, "which could be mimicked by such diminutive insects as [Gulliver]." Was his a valid point? Why?
4. Why did Swift include the king's questions about England in this book?
5. Why do nations keep a standing army in times of peace?
6. Why did Gulliver say he had eluded questions and given points a "more favourable turn" than truth would allow? Have you ever done that? Why?
7. Is it bad to "reduce politics to a science"? What does that mean?

Part 3: A Voyage to Laputa, Balnibarbi, Luggnagg, Glubbdubdrib, and Japan

Review Questions

1. How did Gulliver get to Laputa?
2. What was the role of the flappers on Laputa? Why were they necessary?
3. What did Laputians fear?
4. How did the island of Laputa move? Why was its motion limited?
5. How did the Laputian king punish his subjects?
6. What was odd about the continent ruled by the king of Laputa?
7. Describe the superficies. What was its purpose?
8. How were men at the Academy in Lagado planning to improve language? Why did they fail?
9. How did the doctor in Lagado propose to reconcile violent parties?
10. What was unusual about the governor of Glubbdubdrib's attendants?
11. Which two ancient writers/philosophers did Gulliver first meet on Glubbdubdrib?
12. What was Gulliver's opinion of modern history?

13. What (dis)honor did Gulliver have to perform before coming before the king of Luggnagg?
14. What was unique about the children born with a red spot on their forehead?
15. What happened to the struldbruggs as they aged? What was their quality of life like?
16. What favor did Gulliver ask the Emperor of Japan with regards to the crucifix?

Thought Questions
1. What do math and philosophy have in common? Why are they different from carpentry?
2. What prevents governments from punishing their subjects too severely?
3. Do men value honor and justice while women value constancy and chastity? Discuss.
4. Why could men be their own judges if they were taxed on their virtues? Is this a good idea?
5. Why did Gulliver need to introduce the greats to their critics?
6. Are fraud and perjury "better" flaws than betrayal or perversion of justice?
7. Is ceremony always, to a certain extent, ridiculous? Do people see it that way?
8. Would everlasting, human, earthly life be a gift or a curse?
9. Since Japan is a real place, does this fact change the way you perceive this chapter? Discuss.

Part 4: A Voyage to the Country of the Houyhnhnms

Review Questions
1. How did Gulliver lose his ship?
2. What was unusual about the horses on the island?
3. What were the yahoos? Why did they dismay Gulliver?
4. Why did Gulliver want to hide the fact that he wore clothes?
5. To what "differences of opinion" did Swift/Gulliver attribute European wars?
6. Did England have the capability to produce enough food for all of its people?
7. What was Gulliver's impression of lawyers? Doctors?
8. Did the Houyhnhnms have a classless society?
9. Did Gulliver's master think he was more or less like the yahoos after hearing his stories?
10. What incident convinced Gulliver's master that Gulliver was a real yahoo?
11. On what principles was the culture of the Houyhnhnms based?
12. What question was to be debated at the general assembly of the Houyhnhnms?
13. What did the assembly ask Gulliver's master to do? Why?
14. Where did Gulliver hope to go? Did he want to get back to human society?
15. Who transported Gulliver back to Europe?
16. What was the hardest fault for Gulliver to bear in other yahoos?
17. Why did "Gulliver" write the letter to his cousin Sympson? Of what had he been accused?

Thought Questions
1. Do you view animals as naturally inferior to humans? What makes humans special?
2. What is the effect of having no words to describe lying, doubting, or falsehoods?
3. Is killing worse when it is done by rational creatures?
4. Are laws necessary? Why or why not?

5. Is reason alone enough to govern a rational creature? Why or why not?
6. Gulliver mentioned using yahoo skins to make things. Did this disturb you? Why or why not?
7. Why did Gulliver say this book should be free from censure? To whom was he speaking?
8. What do you think Swift hoped to accomplish with this book?

WRITING REFINEMENT: *Citing Sources*

A court case is nothing without evidence, and a literary essay is the same way. The only real difference is the type of evidence that is suitable. In a literary essay, most of your evidence comes from quotes and examples from the book or poem in question. Sometimes it is best to use direct quotes (using the exact wording and sentence structure of the original), and sometimes you should use paraphrasing (putting the idea into your own words and sentence structure). Either way, when you make a claim, you need to provide evidence.

If you tell someone who has never read *Gulliver's Travels* that the book is a satire, they may ask you how you know. "Because it exaggerates ideas that were considered normal in society, making them seem humorous," you might reply. "Can you give me an example?" is the next logical question.

When you are writing an essay, you should think of your task as a similar conversation. In general, a good writer is as specific as possible in order to answer the reader's questions before they are asked.

Look at the following statements about *Gulliver's Travels*. These are interpretations of the things Swift may have been satirizing. Based on your reading, find 1-3 examples from the book that support each point. If you disagree with one of the statements, find examples that support your position.

Jonathan Swift thought English officials were elected based on the wrong criteria.

Swift thought intellectuals and philosophers can become self-absorbed.

Swift thought modern nations went to war for petty reasons.

Pride and Prejudice
Jane Austen

J ane Austen (1775-1817) was the daughter of an Anglican clergyman in Hampshire, England. After attending boarding school, Austen pursued her own personal interests in reading and writing. Her early writings included short stories, poetry, and plays as well as longer works of fiction. As a mature writer, her social commentaries and subtle satires of English country life earned her esteem. *Pride and Prejudice* is one of her best-known novels. Originally written under the name *First Impressions*, probably around 1799, it was published in 1813. Like many of her books, it was published anonymously in order to avoid the stigma attached to female writers.

UNDERSTANDING LITERATURE:
Devices and Conventions

Jane Austen's books are often classified as "novels of manners", books about the foibles of polite society. Within that social scene, there is a dry sense of humor in Austen's writing and the way she uses dialogue to portray her characters.

Look at the following passage. First, see if you can locate the underlying humor. Second, even without "tags" (he said, she said), can you tell which character is speaking each line? If so, how?

"I have a high respect for your nerves. They are my old friends. I have heard you mention them with consideration these twenty years at least."

"Ah! you do not know what I suffer."

"But I hope you will get over it, and live to see many young men of four thousand a year come into the neighbourhood."

"It will be no use to us if twenty such should come, since you will not visit them."

"Depend upon it, my dear, that when there are twenty I will visit them all."

(Austen 1)

Chapter 1

Review Questions
1. Why was Mrs. Bennet so excited that Netherfield Park had been let?
2. Who was Mr. Bennet's favorite daughter?
3. What was the business of Mrs. Bennet's life?

Thought Questions
1. Are women today as concerned about "marrying off" their daughters? Why or why not?

Chapter 2

Thought Questions
1. Why was Mr. Bennet reluctant to tell his wife that he had visited Mr. Bingley?

Chapter 3

Review Questions
1. Whom did Mr. Bingley bring with him to the ball?
2. Why was Mr. Darcy generally disliked?

Thought Questions
1. Dancing was an important element of society in Austen's time. What has taken its place?

Chapter 4

Thought Questions
1. Compare Elizabeth's and Jane's characters. With which one do you sympathize? Why?
2. Is it strange to form an opinion of someone so quickly (after only two dances)? Discuss.

Chapter 5

Review Questions
1. Who were Elizabeth and Jane's closest friends?

Thought Questions
1. Does anyone have a "right" to be proud? Is there more than one type of pride?

Chapter 6

Review Questions
1. Who took an interest in Elizabeth? What did he first like about her?
2. How did Elizabeth respond when Mr. Darcy asked her to dance?

Thought Questions
1. Do people fall in love without encouragement? What does it mean to fall in love?

2. Is happiness in marriage a matter of chance? Explain.

Chapter 7

Review Questions
1. Who was to inherit Mr. Bennet's estate?
2. What news in Meryton excited the two youngest Bennet girls?
3. What did Miss Bingley write to ask Jane?
4. Why did Mrs. Bennet refuse for Jane to use the carriage? What happened as a result?

Chapter 8

Thought Questions
1. What did "being accomplished" mean to Darcy? What does it mean today?

Chapter 9

Review Questions
1. For what did Darcy criticize the country (as compared to the city)?
2. How did Mrs. Bennet misunderstand his remarks?
3. Why did Mrs. Bennet criticize Charlotte Lucas?

Chapter 10

Thought Questions
1. Is humility, in your opinion, usually genuine? Discuss.
2. What percentage of communication, in your opinion, is misunderstood? Why?
3. Should people ever obey their friends without questioning the reason?

Chapter 11

Review Questions
1. Why did Darcy decline to join Elizabeth and Miss Bingley in walking?
2. What fault in himself did Darcy acknowledge?

Thought Questions
1. Are follies, nonsense, whims, and inconsistencies always weaknesses?
2. Is it a good thing to acknowledge your faults if you do not intend to change them?

Chapter 12

Review Questions
1. Why did Darcy avoid Elizabeth on her last day at Netherfield?

Chapter 13

Review Questions
1. Who came to visit the Bennets?
2. Why had the visitor contacted Mr. Bennet?

Chapter 14

Review Questions
1. Who was Mr. Collins' patroness?
2. Why did Mr. Bennet enjoy listening to Mr. Collins?
3. What type of books did Mr. Collins refuse to read?

Chapter 15

Review Questions
1. What was Mr. Collins' intention in coming to Longbourn?
2. How did he plan to atone for inheriting the estate?
3. What handsome stranger did the Bennet girls meet in town?
4. How did Darcy react upon seeing the girls' new acquaintance?

Chapter 16

Review Questions
1. How was Mr. Wickham connected to Darcy?
2. How did Wickham describe Darcy's sister?
3. How was Lady Catherine de Bourgh related to Darcy?

Chapter 17

Thought Questions
1. Is it wise or right to make excuses for the faults of others, as Jane did?
2. What is your impression of Mary's character? How would you describe her?

Chapter 18

Review Questions
1. Who was notably absent at the ball?
2. What did Miss Bingley tell Elizabeth about Wickham?
3. Who overheard Mrs. Bennet's foolish remarks to Lady Lucas at dinner?

Thought Questions
1. Do you think Elizabeth's judgment of Darcy was fair? Why or why not?
2. Why do you think Mr. Bennet enjoyed his family's awkwardness? Is this an admirable trait?

Chapter 19

Review Questions
1. What were Mr. Collins' reasons for marrying?
2. Why did Mr. Collins not believe Elizabeth's refusal was genuine?

Chapter 20

Review Questions
1. What options did Mr. Bennet give Elizabeth?
2. What finally convinced Mr. Collins to withdraw his proposal?

Chapter 21

Review Questions
1. What news did the letter bring to Jane? Who had sent it?
2. How did Elizabeth interpret the letter's contents?

Chapter 22

Review Questions
1. To whom did Mr. Collins propose? Why did she accept?

Thought Questions
1. Why is marriage no longer the only honorable option for young women without rich parents?

Chapter 23

Review Questions
1. Did Jane hear any news of Mr. Bingley?
2. How did Mrs. Bennet handle the news of Mr. Collins' engagement?

Chapter 24

Thought Questions
1. Do you agree with Elizabeth that all humans are inconstant?
2. Elizabeth said, "You shall not, for the sake of one individual, change the meaning of principle and integrity." Do you agree?

Chapter 25

Review Questions
1. Who were Mr. and Mrs. Gardiner? What did they offer Jane?

Chapter 26

Review Questions
1. Why did Mrs. Gardiner warn Elizabeth against falling in love with Wickham?
2. What favor did Charlotte ask of Elizabeth before she left?
3. How was Jane received in London by Miss Bingley?
4. How and why did Elizabeth and Wickham's flirtation end?

Thought Questions
1. Elizabeth was resigned when Wickham changed his attentions for money, but she was angry at Charlotte for doing the same thing. Was she hypocritical, or were the circumstances different?

Chapter 27

Review Questions
1. Where did Mr. and Mrs. Gardiner invite Elizabeth to go?

Thought Questions
1. What is the difference between being prudent and being mercenary?

Chapter 28

Review Questions
1. Was Charlotte happy with Mr. Collins?
2. Who caused a commotion by stopping at the gate of the parsonage?

Chapter 29

Review Questions
1. What was the whole group invited to do?
2. Describe Lady Catherine. How was she different from her daughter?

Thought Questions
1. Do you agree with Lady Catherine's views on education? Discuss.

Chapter 30

Review Questions
1. What familiar person broke the monotony by coming to visit Rosings?
2. Who was Colonel Fitzwilliam?

Chapter 31

Review Questions
1. Of what did Elizabeth accuse Darcy to Colonel Fitzwilliam?

Thought Questions
1. What did Darcy mean when he told Elizabeth, "We neither of us perform to strangers"?

Chapter 32

Review Questions
1. Who came to call while Elizabeth was alone?
2. What did Charlotte assume to be the reason?
3. What did Elizabeth think about the encounter?

Chapter 33

Review Questions
1. How did Elizabeth interpret her chance encounters with Darcy?
2. What did Colonel Fitzwilliam suggest to Elizabeth about Bingley and Darcy?

Chapter 34

Review Questions
1. What did Darcy confess to Elizabeth? How did she respond?

Thought Questions
1. Is full honesty always best, even if it is offensive?

Chapter 35

Review Questions
1. Why did Darcy approach Elizabeth in the park?
2. Why, according to Darcy, had he come between Jane and Bingley?
3. What did Darcy say about Wickham's story?

Chapter 36

Thought Questions
1. Why do you think Darcy's letter changed Elizabeth's mind about Wickham?
2. Is your character determined by who will vouch for you? Should it be?
3. Should people be judged for their family's behavior?

Chapter 37

Review Questions
1. How did Elizabeth predominantly feel about Darcy?
2. Why was she eager to leave Rosings?

Chapter 38

Review Questions
1. Why did Mr. Collins want Elizabeth to have a favorable impression of his marriage?
2. Where did the travelers stop on the way back to Hertfordshire?

Chapter 39

Review Questions
1. What news about the regiment did Lydia give the sisters when they returned to Hertfordshire?

Chapter 40

Thought Questions
1. Why did Jane want to find a way to see both Wickham and Darcy in a positive light?
2. Should Elizabeth have publicly exposed Wickham's bad character? Why or why not?

Chapter 41

Review Questions
1. What invitation did Mrs. Forster issue to Lydia?
2. What did Elizabeth tell Wickham to disquiet him on their last meeting? How did he respond?

Thought Questions
1. Do you agree with Mr. Bennet's or Elizabeth's opinion about Lydia's absurdity?

Chapter 42

Review Questions
1. What did Elizabeth learn about marriage from her family?
2. Where did Elizabeth's aunt and uncle take her?

Thought Questions
1. What were Mr. Bennet's failings as a husband?
2. On what do you base your ideas of marriage: Your peers? Your family? Media?

Chapter 43

Review Questions
1. What did Darcy's housekeeper think of him?
2. Whom did Darcy want Elizabeth to meet?

Thought Questions
1. Do you think having a servant's praise is particularly commendable? If so, why?

Chapter 44

Review Questions
1. Describe Miss Darcy.
2. Who else came to visit Elizabeth?
3. How had Darcy changed since Elizabeth saw him in Hunsford?

Thought Questions
1. Is love different from gratitude?

Chapter 45

Review Questions
1. Who attempted to disparage Elizabeth to Darcy and his sister?

Chapter 46

Review Questions
1. What disturbing news did Jane's letter contain?
2. What did the letter ask Elizabeth to do?

Thought Questions
1. Could the crisis have been prevented if Elizabeth had warned her family about Wickham?
2. Which is a better foundation for attachment, gratitude or initial attraction?

Chapter 47

Review Questions
1. Why did the family assume Wickham did not intend to marry Lydia?
2. Who was to blame for the situation?

Chapter 48

Review Questions
1. What did Mr. Collins write to advise Mr. Bennet?
2. What new discipline policy did Mr. Bennet propose for Kitty?

Chapter 49

Review Questions
1. What news came from Mr. Gardiner?
2. Why did Mr. Bennet think Mr. Gardiner had paid money to Wickham?

Chapter 50

Review Questions
1. What house did Mr. Bennet declare Lydia and Wickham could never enter?
2. What new information did Mr. Gardiner send?

Chapter 51

Review Questions
1. Did Lydia's manner change as a result of the scandal?
2. What did Lydia tell Elizabeth about the people who had attended her marriage?

Chapter 52

Review Questions
1. How did Mrs. Gardiner explain the situation surrounding Lydia's marriage?
2. What role had Darcy played in the affair?
3. Why did Wickham approach Elizabeth in the park?

Chapter 53

Review Questions
1. What news restored Mrs. Bennet's humor after Lydia and Wickham left?
2. How were the visitors received?

Chapter 54

Thought Questions
1. Should Elizabeth have told her mother what the family owed Darcy?
2. What would it take for a man to propose twice to the same person?
3. Would such an action be foolish or persistent? Discuss.

Chapter 55

Review Questions
1. How did Bingley propose?

Chapter 56

Review Questions
1. Which unlikely visitor came to Longbourn?

    2. Why had she come?

Thought Questions
    1. Are families an important consideration in choosing whom to marry?
    2. Is it important to have your family's consent?

Chapter 57

Review Questions
    1. Why did Mr. Collins write to Mr. Bennet?

Thought Questions
    1. How did Mr. Collins define Christian forgiveness? Do you agree?

Chapter 58

Review Questions
    1. What did Elizabeth reveal to Darcy while they were walking?
    2. How did Darcy explain his generosity to the family?
    3. What gave Darcy the courage to speak to Elizabeth?

Thought Questions
    1. What do you think was Elizabeth's greatest fault? Darcy's?
    2. In what way do you think Elizabeth changed the most? Darcy?
    3. Which proposal took greater courage, Bingley's or Darcy's? Why?

Chapter 59

Review Questions
    1. Why did Elizabeth hesitate to tell her family about her engagement?
    2. Why did Mr. Bennet oppose the marriage?
    3. How did Mrs. Bennet respond?

Thought Questions
    1. Jane said, "Do anything rather than marry without affection." Is this good advice?

Chapter 60

Review questions
    1. Why did Charlotte and Mr. Collins come to visit the Lucases?

Thought Questions
    1. What is the difference between impertinence and a lively mind? Is there one?

Chapter 61

Review Questions
    1. Did marrying off three daughters improve Mrs. Bennet's character?
    2. What did Lydia hope to gain from Elizabeth and Darcy's marriage?
    3. How did Kitty benefit from the marriage?

Thought Questions
    1. Discuss Mr. Bennet's humor and sarcasm. Do you like his character? Why or why not?

2. Why do you think Austen ended by neatly wrapping up each of the characters' lives?
3. Discuss Austen's use of dialogue to develop her characters. Is this effective?

WRITING REFINEMENT:
Citing Sources

Inserting quotations from a book into an essay in a smooth and correct fashion can be difficult when you are dealing with a quote that contains dialogue. Look at the following paragraph, a sample of the type you might use in an essay on *Pride and Prejudice*. From the two quotations below, choose one you think is most appropriate to back up the paragraph's argument, and insert it, using correct format. Remember to use single quotation marks (' ') to show dialogue within a quote, and regular quotation marks (" ") to set off the whole quote.

Paragraph

In *Pride and Prejudice*, Lady Catherine de Bourgh provides one of the key elements in Elizabeth and Darcy's eventual marriage. By challenging Elizabeth's right to have Darcy, she helps Elizabeth realize how much she loves him. Although Lady Catherine does not intend for this to happen, her pride is actually necessary for the book's happy ending.

1. "Lady Catherine approached, and, after listening for a few minutes, said to Darcy, 'Miss Bennet would not play at all amiss, if she practised more' […] Elizabeth looked at Darcy to see how cordially he assented to his cousin's praise; but neither at that moment nor at any other could she discern any symptom of love."

2. "'Your alliance will be a disgrace; your name will never even be mentioned by any of us.' 'These are heavy misfortunes,' replied Elizabeth. 'But the wife of Mr. Darcy must have such extraordinary sources of happiness necessarily attached to her situation, that she could, upon the whole, have no cause to repine'."

A Tale of Two Cities
Charles Dickens

Charles Dickens (1812-1870) was born in London, and at the age of twelve, he was forced to work in a factory to pay off family debts while his father was in debtor's prison. Dickens received minimal formal schooling, and then he worked as a law clerk and stenographer before becoming a freelance journalist in 1834, and later a literary editor. From there, Dickens turned to writing of a different nature, producing humorous sketches as well as the novels that have made his name famous. Dickens was also dedicated to amateur theatre, and he gave frequent public readings from his own works. *A Tale of Two Cities* was published in 1859 as a weekly serial in *All the Year Round*.

UNDERSTANDING LITERATURE:
Devices and Conventions

A Tale of Two Cities is set apart by several distinct characteristics. First, the novel was originally written in serial form. It appeared in installments in a weekly journal. Readers could only see a piece at a time. Second, *A Tale of Two Cities* makes good use of narration techniques. The book is narrated in **third person omniscient**. The **narrator** knows things that the characters do not and can analyze the entire situation, which the characters cannot see. The narrator uses this feature to create **irony**.

A Tale of Two Cities is built on contrasts and seeming contradictions. The book begins, "It was the best of times, it was the worst of times," showing the two-sided nature of the time period. Examine the two quotes and scenarios below. What is ironic—in other words, what seems contradictory—about the statement in light of the situation?

1. "'For gracious sake, don't talk about Liberty; we have quite enough of that,' said Miss Pross" (287). The family lived in a small flat in Paris, and, for safety, Miss Pross ran their daily errands.

2. "'The Republic goes before all. The People is supreme'" (290). Freed only recently by the will of the people, Charles was rearrested because he had been denounced by one man and his wife.

Book 1: Recalled to Life
Chapter 1: The Period

Review Questions
1. Choose two words that you think describe this time period. Why did you choose them?

Chapter 2: The Mail

Review Questions
1. Who was travelling by Dover road?
2. For whom was the messenger looking?
3. What message was sent in reply?

Chapter 3: The Night Shadows

Review Questions
1. Did Jerry understand the message?
2. What did Mr. Lorry dream in the coach?

Chapter 4: The Preparation

Review Questions
1. Who arrived to see Mr. Lorry at the inn in Dover?
2. Why had Mr. Lorry been sent to meet her?
3. What had happened to Monsieur Manette?

Chapter 5: The Wine Shop

Review Questions
1. Were conditions in France good for the common person?
2. Why did Mr. Lorry and Miss Manette visit the wine shop?
3. What did M. Defarge show them in the garret?

Thought Questions
1. Why do you think Dickens included the incident of the wine cask breaking? What did it reveal about the French people?

Chapter 6: The Shoemaker

Review Questions
1. Did M. Manette recognize his daughter? If so, how?
2. Where did Mr. Lorry and Miss Manette take M. Manette?

Thought Questions
1. Why did Mr. Lorry need to ask, "I hope you care to be recalled to life?"

Book 2: The Golden Thread
Chapter 1: Five Years Later

Review Questions

1. Describe Tellson's bank.
2. How did Mr. Cruncher earn a living?

Chapter 2: A Sight

Review Questions
1. What did the bank hire Mr. Cruncher to do?
2. What was Old Bailey?
3. Who was the prisoner? With what was he charged?

Chapter 3: A Disappointment

Review Questions
1. What two men accused the prisoner? How were the witnesses discredited?
2. Why were the Manettes at the trial?
3. What was strange about the wigged man at the trial? How did he influence the outcome?
4. What was the jury's decision?

Thought Questions
1. Was this an example of a fair trial? Why or why not?

Chapter 4: Congratulatory

Review Questions
1. What kind of man was Mr. Carton, in your estimation?
2. How did Mr. Carton feel about Mr. Darnay? How do you know?

Chapter 5: The Jackal

Review Questions
1. Why was Mr. Carton compared to a jackal?
2. To what did Mr. Carton attribute his lack of achievement and status in the world?

Thought Questions
1. At what point does a life become "wasted"? Is this situation always avoidable?

Chapter 6: Hundreds of People

Review Questions
1. Why was Miss Pross frustrated about Lucie Manette?
2. What did Mr. Lorry find curious about Dr. Manette's relationship with the past?
3. What story did Darnay tell about the carvings in the dungeon? How did Dr. Manette react?

Thought Questions
1. Why do you think Dr. Manette kept the shoemaker's tools?

Chapter 7: Monseigneur in Town

Review Questions
1. Who demonstrated scorn toward Monseigneur by shaking snuff off his fingers?
2. What did M. le Marquis' carriage hit?

Thought Questions
1. Why do you think Dickens described the routine of Monseigneur's morning chocolate?

Chapter 8: Monseigneur in the Country

Review Questions
1. What had one of the poor men observed as Monseigneur's carriage travelled downhill?
2. What did the poor woman ask of Monseigneur?

Chapter 9: The Gorgon's Head

Review Questions
1. Who was the Marquis' nephew?
2. Why did the Marquis' nephew choose to renounce his inheritance?
3. What happened to M. le Marquis?

Thought Questions
1. "Detestation of the high is the involuntary homage of the low." What does this mean? Do you agree?
2. "Repression is the only lasting philosophy." Discuss this quotation. Do you agree? Why or why not?

Chapter 10: Two Promises

Review Questions
1. What was Darnay's employment?
2. Why did he not reveal his love for Lucie? How did Dr. Manette respond when he did?
3. Who were Lucie's other potential suitors?
4. What did Darnay offer the doctor in exchange for his promise of support?

Chapter 11: A Companion Picture

Review Questions
1. What plan did Mr. Stryver reveal to Carton?

Chapter 12: The Fellow of Delicacy

Review Questions
1. Did Mr. Stryver expect Miss Manette to agree?
2. Why did Mr. Lorry discourage him?
3. Why did Mr. Stryver "change his mind" about the advisability of the match?

Chapter 13: The Fellow of No Delicacy

Review Questions
1. What did Carton tell Lucie?
2. What three things did he ask her to do?

Thought Questions
1. "I am like one who died young. All my life might have been." What does this mean?

2. Do you know people who feel like this? Does it have to be this way?

Chapter 14: The Honest Tradesman

Review Questions
1. Whose funeral procession passed by Jerry Cruncher?
2. For what did Jerry go "fishing"?

Thought Questions
1. Discuss Jerry's treatment of his wife. Do you think he was fair? Why or why not?

Chapter 15: Knitting

Review Questions
1. What happened to the tall man who had hung from M. le Marquis' brake?
2. How did Madame Defarge keep the register of rebels?

Thought Questions
1. What was the significance of the women's knitting? Was it sinister or good?
2. Why did all the conspirators go by the name of Jacques?

Chapter 16: Still Knitting

Review Questions
1. Why did John Barsad visit the Defarges' wine shop? What did he reveal to the Defarges?
2. What did Madame Defarge do in response?

Thought Questions
1. Discuss the quotation, "Vengeance and retribution require a long time; it is the rule." Does this mean vengeance takes a long time to take place or to satisfy?
2. Would you describe Mme. Defarge as a great or grand woman? Why or why not?

Chapter 17: One Night

Review Questions
1. Was Dr. Manette happy about Lucie's marriage?

Thought Questions
1. Is it a good thing or a bad thing to remember unpleasant times?

Chapter 18: Nine Days

Review Questions
1. What happened to upset Dr. Manette on Lucie and Charles' wedding day?
2. What did Dr. Manette do after the couple left on their honeymoon?

Chapter 19: An Opinion

Review Questions
1. How did Dr. Manette explain his relapse and recovery?
2. Why did Mr. Lorry want to take away the shoemaker's bench?

Chapter 20: A Plea

Review Questions
1. Why did Carton want to be friends with Darnay?
2. What did Lucie ask Darnay on Carton's behalf?

Chapter 21: Echoing Footsteps

Review Questions
1. What was happening in St. Antoine in 1789?
2. What was 105 North Tower? What did Defarge find there?
3. What did the people do to the governor?

Thought Questions
1. Why do you think Lucie's children liked Carton?
2. How would you categorize the storming of the Bastille: Cruel? Noble? Glorious? Why?

Chapter 22: The Sea Still Rises

Review Questions
1. Who was Old Foulon? What did the mob do to him, and why?

Chapter 23: Fire Rises

Review Questions
1. What happened to the village near Monseigneur's chateau?

Chapter 24: Drawn to the Loadstone Rock

Review Questions
1. Why did Mr. Lorry intend to go to France? Whom did Charles Darnay propose to send instead?
2. Who was the Marquis de St. Evrémonde?
3. What did the letter ask Darnay to do?

Thought Questions
1. Do you think Darnay had more of an obligation to Lucie or to Gabelle? Why?
2. Did he make the right choice?

Book 3: The Track of a Storm

Chapter 1: In Secret

Review Questions
1. What was the slogan of the French Revolution?
2. What decree had been passed the same day Darnay left England?
3. Was it easier to get in or out of Paris?
4. What sentence was pronounced on Darnay at the Paris gate? Who escorted him from the gate?
5. What did "in secret" mean?

Thought Questions
1. Discuss the slogan of the French Revolution. Is it right to kill in the name of liberty?

2. Why was "La Guillotine" discussed in female terms?

Chapter 2: The Grindstone

Review Questions
1. Who rushed into Tellson's of Paris to see Mr. Lorry in the middle of the night?
2. What was happening in the courtyard that Lorry did not want Lucie to see?
3. Who went to rescue Darnay?

Chapter 3: The Shadow

Review Questions
1. What message did Defarge bring Mr. Lorry?

Thought Questions
1. Why were Mme. Defarge and The Vengeance said to have a shadow?

Chapter 4: Calm in Storm

Review Questions
1. How did Dr. Manette handle the strain of protecting Darnay?

Thought Questions
1. Does injustice always accompany revolution? Discuss.

Chapter 5: The Wood-Sawyer

Review Questions
1. Why did Lucie stand daily by the wood-cutter's house?
2. What was the Carmagnole?

Chapter 6: Triumph

Review Questions
1. What was Darnay's defense before the court?
2. What was the verdict?

Chapter 7: A Knock at the Door
1. Who did the daily shopping for Lucie and her family?
2. Who knocked at the door that night?
3. Who had denounced Darnay?

Chapter 8: A Hand at Cards

Review Questions
1. Whom did Miss Pross and Mr. Cruncher meet at the wine shop?
2. By what other name was the man known? Who supplied this other name?
3. How did Mr. Cruncher know Barsad was lying about his old partner?

Chapter 9: The Game Made

Review Questions

1. What promise had Carton won from Barsad?
2. Where did Carton go after he left Mr. Lorry?
3. Who was the third person said to have denounced Darnay?
4. What was Defarge's evidence?

Thought Questions
1. Is life worthless if it is not filled with human love, respect, or attachments?
2. What is your impression of Sydney Carton's character? Is he noble? Tragic?
3. Can a revolution take place if laws and ceremonies are not destroyed?

Chapter 10: The Substance of the Shadow

Review Questions
1. In the letter, why had Dr. Manette been taken in the carriage?
2. Who were the two patients? What had happened to them?
3. To what family did the two young noblemen belong?
4. Why had Dr. Manette been imprisoned?
5. What was Darnay's sentence?

Chapter 11: Dusk

Review Questions
1. Who carried Lucie from the courthouse?

Thought Questions
1. Do you think it was hard for Dr. Manette to accept Charles as a son-in-law? Why or why not?
2. "Of little worth as life is when we misuse it, it is worth that effort. It would cost nothing to lay down if it were not." Discuss.

Chapter 12: Darkness

Review Questions
1. Why did Carton go to Defarge's wine shop?
2. What further harm did Mme. Defarge intend to do? Why?
3. What did Dr. Manette ask for when he returned in the morning?
4. What did Carton tell Mr. Lorry to do?
5. What did he make Mr. Lorry promise?

Chapter 13: Fifty-two

Review Questions
1. How did Darnay remain calm while waiting to die?
2. What did Carton tell Darnay to do?
3. What did he tell Darnay to write? What did Carton do while Darnay was writing?

Chapter 14: The Knitting Done

Review Questions
1. Did Mme. Defarge decide to spare Dr. Manette?
2. Why did Miss Pross and Mr. Cruncher not leave with the rest?
3. What was the result of Mme. Defarge and Miss Pross's encounter?

Thought Questions
1. Are Mme. Defarge's actions and sentiments understandable in light of her past? Are they excusable?

Chapter 15: The Footsteps Die Out For Ever

Review Questions
1. Looking back, of whom was Carton speaking, at the end of chapter 11, when he said, "Otherwise she might think 'his life was wantonly thrown away or wasted'"?
2. How did Carton handle his death?

Thought Questions
1. Was the French Revolution inevitable? Was the American?
2. Look at the last lines of the book. Do you think Carton redeemed himself at the end, or had he already done so?

WRITING REFINEMENT:
Using the Vocabulary

Knowing literary terminology not only improves your vocabulary, it also gives you specific and correct words to use when you talk about literature. Look at the list of words below and choose the best word to replace the underlined words in the paragraph below. (If you are not sure of the meaning of these terms, look back at "Using the Vocabulary" in the "Writing Refinement" section at the beginning of this book.) Each word is only used once, and not all of the words are used.

Internal conflict	External conflict	Point of view
Plot	Climax	Narrator
Protagonist(s)	Antagonist(s)	Foreshadows
Frames	Alludes	

In *A Tale of Two Cities*, Dickens begins with the French Revolution. He uses the close proximity of London and Paris to create tension for his main characters. By creating two characters who are in love with the same woman, Dickens begins with personal problems and builds to the issues of loyalty and justice to create large-scale problems. All of the main characters—Sydney Carton, Charles Darnay, and Lucie Manette—are affected by these problems, which form Dickens' storyline. Because Dickens creates believable, flawed characters, it is difficult to determine who the villain is. The case of mistaken identity at the beginning of the book hints at the idea that the relationship between Darnay and Carton will be a key point later in the book. As the story builds toward a turning point, the tension between the two men continues to escalate.

Jane Eyre
Charlotte Brontë

Charlotte Brontë (1816-1855) was one of three writing sisters in the Brontë family, along with Emily and Ann. Their early writings were about an imaginary world they called Angria. In addition to writing, Charlotte served as a teacher and a governess in England and also in Brussels, Belgium. Her literary career was closely tied to those of her sisters. In 1846, the Brontë sisters published their first collection of poetry. Wishing to avoid gender stereotypes, each one published under a masculine pseudonym: Emily was Ellis Bell, Ann was Acton Bell, and Charlotte was Currer Bell. In 1847, Charlotte published the novel *Jane Eyre*, Ann published *Agnes Grey*, and Emily published *Wuthering Heights*. Although the novels became quite popular, the authors' true identities were not revealed until 1848. After Emily's and Ann's deaths, Charlotte went on to write two more novels.

UNDERSTANDING LITERATURE:
Devices and Conventions

Jane Eyre is a dark book with some of the characteristics of a gothic novel. (Gothic novels are characterized by a pervasive sense of mystery and gloom. They are often set in old, sometimes haunted buildings and deal with themes of madness, secrecy, and supernatural events.) The use of **first person** narration makes the book a personal account of Jane's life. The **allusions** to other literary works and the strategic use of French create a sense of refinement and education. The mood of *Jane Eyre* is influenced by these things, but word choice also plays an important role.

Look at the following two passages from the book. The first describes Jane's first impression of Thornfield. The second is her first impression of Mr. Rochester. Write down a few words that describe the mood of the selection. Then go back through the passage and pick out the words that contributed to your perception of mood.

1. "About ten minutes after, the driver got down and opened a pair of gates; we

passed through, and they clashed to behind us. We now slowly ascended a drive, and came upon the long front of a house; candlelight gleamed from one curtained bow-window; all the rest were dark." (Brontë 97).

2. "He had a dark face, with stern features and a heavy brow; his eyes and gathered eyebrows looked ireful and thwarted just now…" (117).

When Jane described Mr. Rochester, did she mean his forehead literally weighed a lot? What did she mean? What other words in the passage are used in a way that is not literal? Think about the way that figurative language contributes to the mood of literature.

Chapter 1

Review Questions
1. What was Jane's relationship to the Reeds?
2. Did Jane like living with the Reeds? Why or why not?

Chapter 2

Review Questions
1. Why did Jane attack Jack?
2. Why did Jane scream when she was locked in her room?
3. How did Mrs. Reed interpret her plea?

Chapter 3

Review Questions
1. What did Mr. Lloyd recommend be done with Jane?

Thought Questions
1. When does poverty become shameful?

Chapter 4

Review Questions
1. Who came to take Jane away from the Reeds? Where was he going to take her?
2. What did Jane tell Mrs. Reed before she left?

Thought Questions
1. Mr. Brocklehurst told a story about a boy who preferred Scripture to ginger-nuts. Look at this story. Do you think the story proved his point? If not, how would you interpret the story?
2. Was it right for Mrs. Reed to tell Mr. Brocklehurst bad things about Jane to "prepare him"? Why or why not?
3. Mrs. Reed advocated consistency. Was she consistent?

Chapter 5

Review Questions
1. What was Lowood Institution?
2. How was Jane treated at Lowood?

Chapter 6

Review Questions
1. Who was Helen Burns? How was she treated by the teachers at Lowood?

Thought Questions
1. What was Helen's "doctrine of endurance"? Do you agree with her? Why or why not?
2. Jane said if you are good to cruel people, they will never change. Discuss this philosophy.

Chapter 7

Review Questions
1. Why did Jane dread Mr. Brocklehurst's visit?
2. What happened to Jane when he came?

Chapter 8

Review Questions
1. Who defended Jane to the rest of the school?

Chapter 9

Review Questions
1. Why was the school transformed into a hospital in the spring?
2. What happened to Helen Burns?

Thought Questions
1. How did Helen define God? Do you think her description was accurate?

Chapter 10

Review Questions
1. Why did Miss Temple leave Lowood?
2. Where did Jane plan to go when she left Lowood?

Chapter 11

Review Questions
1. What was the situation at Thornfield? Who owned it?
2. Who was Jane's pupil? What was her situation?
3. What did Jane hear in the attic? Who was Grace Poole?

Thought Questions
1. What makes someone "accomplished"? How have expectations changed?

Chapter 12

Review Questions
1. How did Jane meet Mr. Rochester?

Chapter 13

Review Questions
1. Why did Jane like Mr. Rochester?
2. How did Mrs. Fairfax explain Mr. Rochester's peculiarities?

Chapter 14

Thought Questions
1. Does age always produce superiority? In what sense?
2. Can an action be made right by pronouncing it so?

Chapter 15

Review Questions
1. Who was Adele's mother? How was she related to Mr. Rochester?
2. What happened to disturb Jane's sleep?
3. What did Jane discover when she investigated the disturbance?
4. How did Mr. Rochester respond to that night's events?

Chapter 16

Review Questions
1. Where did Mr. Rochester go?
2. What two portraits did Jane draw?

Chapter 17

Review Questions
1. What conversation did Jane overhear between Leah and the charwoman? What did it mean?
2. Did Blanche Ingram match up to Jane's painting?

Thought Questions
1. What were Jane's feelings for Mr. Rochester? When did she discover them?

Chapter 18

Thought Questions
1. Is there something innately wrong with marrying for money or connections?
2. Why do people marry today?

Chapter 19

Review Questions
1. Who was Old Mother Bunches? What was unusual about her?
2. What did she tell Jane?

Thought Questions
1. What, if anything, do you think Mr. Rochester learned from his trick?

Chapter 20

Review Questions
1. What happened to Mr. Mason?
2. What strange command did Mr. Rochester give him and Jane?
3. What story did he tell Jane in the garden? How did it relate to his situation?

Thought Questions
1. What is the difference between an error and a crime?
2. How would you categorize Mr. Rochester's experience?

Chapter 21

Review Questions
1. What news did Robert Leaven bring?
2. What did he ask Jane to do?
3. Why did Jane ask to leave Thornfield temporarily?
4. How was she received?
5. What wrongs had Mrs. Reed done to Jane?

Thought Questions
1. Why do you think Mrs. Reed wanted to see Jane before she died?

Chapter 22

Review Questions
1. What did Jane find when she returned to Thornfield?

Chapter 23

Review Questions
1. What did Mr. Rochester ask Jane?

Thought Questions
1. Why do you think Mr. Rochester wanted to marry Jane?
2. Was there any significance to the horse-chestnut tree being struck by lightning after Jane and Mr. Rochester's conversation?

Chapter 24

Review Questions
1. What did Jane ask Mr. Rochester to do? What was his response?

Thought Questions
1. What characterized Jane and Mr. Rochester's relationship? Would you call it healthy?

Chapter 25

Review Questions
1. What had happened to make Jane uneasy a few nights before her wedding?
2. How did Mr. Rochester explain the occurrence?

Chapter 26

Review Questions
1. What disrupted Jane and Mr. Rochester's marriage?
2. Who was Bertha Mason?
3. How did Mr. Mason know Jane's uncle?

Thought Questions
1. Was Mr. Rochester's treatment of Bertha ethical?

Chapter 27

Review Questions
1. What did Mr. Rochester ask Jane to do? What was her answer? Why?
2. Why did Mr. Rochester think his first marriage was not genuine?

Thought Questions
1. "Friends always forget those whom fortune forsakes." Do you agree?
2. Was Jane right to refuse Mr. Rochester's offer? Discuss the logic of his plea?
3. Is monogamy a "mere human law"? Is anyone hurt by its disregard?

Chapter 28

Review Questions
1. Where did Jane go when she left Thornfield?
2. How was Jane generally received in the village?
3. Where did Jane spend the night? With whom?

Thought Questions
1. How would you respond if you were in the villagers' place when Jane asked for help?

Chapter 29

Review Questions
1. What did Jane ask the Rivers to do for her?

Chapter 30

Review Questions
1. What employment did St. John offer Jane? Did she accept?
2. What news did the letter bring to the Rivers?

Chapter 31

Review Questions
1. What prevented St. John from loving Miss Oliver?

Thought Questions
1. Which fate would you choose, "to be a slave in a fool's paradise" or "to be a village-schoolmistress, free and honest"? Why?

Chapter 32

Review Questions
1. Why did Jane offer St. John a copy of Rosamond's portrait? Did he accept it?
2. What did St. John take with him when he left the cottage?

Thought Questions
1. How would you describe St. John's concept of Christianity?

Chapter 33

Review Questions
1. Why did St. John return the following day? What story did he tell Jane?
2. How did he know Jane's real name?
3. Why was Mr. Briggs looking for her?
4. How was St. John related to Jane?
5. What did Jane decide to do with the inheritance?

Chapter 34

Review Questions
1. What did St. John ask Jane? Why did he want her to learn Hindostanee?

Thought Questions
1. Is it wrong, like St. John, to be too aspiring?
2. If you are capable of something, are you obliged to do it? Should you be?
3. What is wrong with marriage that does not involve love?

Chapter 35

Review Questions
1. How did St. John respond to Jane's refusal?
2. What occurrence kept Jane from giving in to St. John's wishes?

Thought Questions
1. Is it symbolic that Mr. Rivers' name is St. John? Discuss.

Chapter 36

Review Questions
1. Why did Jane return to Thornfield?
2. What did she find when she returned? What had happened?
3. What had happened to Bertha?
4. What had happened to Mr. Rochester?

Chapter 37

Review Questions
1. Where did Jane find Mr. Rochester?
2. How did Mr. Rochester misunderstand Jane's offer to stay with him?
3. What was her intention?
4. How had Mr. Rochester's view of God changed as a result of his affliction?
5. What strange occurrence had given him renewed hope?

Thought Questions
1. What, if anything, do you think Mr. Rochester lost along with his sight?
2. Why do you think Jane still called Mr. Rochester "master"?
3. How would you interpret Mr. Rochester and Jane's supernatural "meeting"?

Chapter 38

Review Questions
1. How did Mr. Rochester regain his sight?

Thought Questions
1. Why do you think Brontë ended the book with St. John's last words?

WRITING REFINEMENT:
Practicing Clarity, Precision, and Sophistication

Improving your vocabulary is an important step in becoming a more precise, sophisticated writer. *Jane Eyre* is an excellent book to read if you want to improve your vocabulary. The words Brontë chose to tell her story are both complex and precise. As you look at the following list of words from the book, use your knowledge of other words to guess at the root meaning of each word. Then use a dictionary to confirm or correct your original idea.

Opprobrium	Ignominy
Vassalage	Homily
Usurious	Expostulation
Hebdomadal	Quiescence
Salubrious	Equipage
Lugubrious	Contumacy
Ebullition	Oblation
Propitiate	Lineaments
Acrimony	Puerile
Cicatrized	Ruth
Lachrymose	

Animal Farm
George Orwell

Eric Arthur Blair (1903-1950), better known by his pen name George Orwell, was born in India during British imperial control. After finishing school, he served for five years in the Indian Imperial Police. This experience strengthened his dislike of empire, a fact reflected in his early essays and short stories. Always interested in the links between literature and politics, Orwell became strongly anti-fascist in later years. He fought in the Spanish Civil War and served as a war correspondent during World War II, but he continued to write fiction as well. He is best known for two novels speaking against totalitarianism: *Animal Farm* was published in 1945, and *1984* followed in 1949.

UNDERSTANDING LITERATURE:
Genre

Animal Farm is a difficult book to categorize for several reasons. It has been categorized as an allegory, a fairy tale, a beast fable, and a satire. Below are some of the characteristics of each of these genres.

Allegory

A story in which characters and places represent something, usually an abstract idea
Names are significant as predictors of character

Fairy Tale

A story about the adventures and mischief of spirits living or working among men
Contains surreal qualities such as talking animals, witches, and magic

Beast Fable

A story with a definitive moral
The characters are talking animals

Satire

     A story in which humor is used to encourage reform

     Concepts and ideas are taken to the extreme to expose their flaws

As you read, jot down characteristics of the book that fit or do not fit each category. After you have finished reading, decide which category you think is most appropriate.

Chapter 1

Review Questions

1. What did the animals gather to hear after Mr. Jones went to bed?
2. Did Major think the animals' suffering was natural?
3. What, in Major's eyes, separated man from the other creatures?
4. What did Major encourage the animals to do?

Thought Questions

1. Discuss the logic of the argument, "All men are enemies," and "All animals are friends."
2. Why was it important for the animals not to resemble man after conquering him?
3. What was the basic message of "Beasts of England"? Why are patriotic songs so powerful?

Chapter 2

Review Questions

1. Which two animals led the rebellion movement?
2. What was Squealer's talent?
3. On what grounds did Moses argue against the revolution?
4. When and how was the rebellion achieved?
5. What were the basic tenets of Animalism?

Thought Questions

1. On the basis of the initial description, which leader would you be more inclined to follow? Why?
2. Is it a compliment to call someone a "brilliant talker"? Why or why not?
3. Can rebellion occur without a sudden uprising or outpouring of emotion? Discuss.
4. Discuss the seven commandments of Animalism. Are they just? Fair? Good? What basis are you using to judge them?

Chapter 3

Review Questions

1. Did the work go better or worse without Jones?
2. What was Boxer's motto?
3. What did the colors and designs on the flag represent?
4. To what did Snowball reduce the seven commandments? Do you think his was an accurate rendering of the principles of Animalism?
5. What privileges were the pigs given?

Thought Questions
1. "Donkeys live a long time. None of you has ever seen a dead donkey." What does this mean?
2. Discuss the character of the cat. What role did it play in the story?

Chapter 4

Review Questions
1. What two farms bordered Animal Farm? Who were the owners?
2. How did the success of Animal Farm affect the nearby farms?
3. When the pigeons came to Animal Farm in October, what news did they bring?
4. Who led the response?

Thought Questions
1. Discuss Boxer's unwillingness to take human life. Was he a pacifist? What are the most basic arguments for and against pacifism?

Chapter 5

Review Questions
1. How did Mollie cause trouble? What was her most serious offense? Where did she go?
2. What controversy arose over the windmill?
3. What differing positions did Snowball and Napoleon take on the farm's defense?
4. What interrupted the vote about the windmill?
5. What changes did Napoleon institute?
6. What new maxim did Boxer adopt?
7. How did Squealer describe tactics? Give an example.

Thought Questions
1. Why were Mollie's actions seen as a betrayal?
2. Why do factions and organizations always have slogans? What is the point of a slogan?
3. Which is more important in decision-making, efficiency or democracy?

Chapter 6

Review Questions
1. How did the animals break up stone for the windmill?
2. What new policy did Napoleon devise in order to acquire things the animals could not make?
3. How did Squealer explain the pigs' move into the farmhouse?
4. How had the fourth commandment changed?
5. What happened to the windmill? What was Napoleon's explanation?

Thought Questions
1. Was the animals' need for things they could not produce inevitable?
2. If something you want to do is wrong, one way around it is to change the rule. Discuss the consequences of and logic behind such an action.

Chapter 7

Review Questions
1. Why did the animals try to hide their lack of food?
2. Why did the hens revolt? What were the consequences?
3. How did Napoleon use Snowball's name? What did he gain by doing so?
4. What happened at the assembly?
5. Why did Napoleon abolish "Beasts of England"? Distinguish between stated and actual reasons.

Thought Questions
1. Why was the bloodshed more disturbing to the animals than it was when Jones ran the farm?

Chapter 8

Review Questions
1. How had the sixth commandment changed?
2. Describe the negotiations between Napoleon, Pilkington, and Frederick.
3. To whom did Napoleon sell the timber?
4. How were the animals betrayed?
5. What did the attackers do to the windmill?
6. How did Squealer redefine the results of the battle?
7. How was the fifth commandment changed? Why?

Thought Questions
1. Why did the animals attribute to Napoleon things that were outside his control?
2. Why do you think animals confessed to secret plots if they were not guilty?

Chapter 9

Review Questions
1. Did the animals have a retirement plan?
2. What was a "Spontaneous Demonstration"? What was the point?
3. Why did Boxer collapse? Where was he supposedly sent? Where was he actually sent?
4. How did the pigs get money for more whisky?

Thought Questions
1. How does word choice change perceptions? Do "readjustment" and "reduction" refer to the same action?
2. Do words like "free," "better," "more," and "dignity" have a concrete meaning?
3. What did Moses represent? Why do you think he came back? Why did the pigs tolerate him?
4. Why was Boxer's death a turning point for Animal Farm? What did it symbolize?

Chapter 10

Review Questions
1. How was the windmill used?
2. What kind of lifestyle did Napoleon advocate as in the "spirit of Animalism"?
3. Did the pigs and dogs work?
4. What new behavior did the pigs take on?

5. What prevented the other animals from protesting?
6. What happened to the seven commandments?
7. What did the other animals see when they looked in the farmhouse windows?

Thought Questions
1. Why do you think Benjamin was the only animal who did not change?
2. Is disappointment, as Benjamin suggested, "the unalterable law of life"? Discuss.
3. Why was it significant that the pigs and the humans looked alike?

WRITING REFINEMENT: *Analyzing Influences*

Orwell was noted for his strong opinions about politics and political philosophies. He experienced first-hand the impact of totalitarianism in the Spanish Civil War, and he feared its spread during World War II. In order to write more effectively about and accurately assess the political connections in Orwell's novels, you should know more about totalitarianism and other political ideas that were current when Orwell was writing.

Using the Internet or a library, find one credible source discussing each of the following ideas: totalitarianism, communism, and fascism. Look especially for information about the application of these ideas during the Spanish Civil War and World War II and in the U.S.S.R. Based on your research, do you think Orwell was referring to these philosophies in *Animal Farm*? If so, which ones? Keep in mind the date when *Animal Farm* was published.

A Christmas Carol
Charles Dickens

On December 18, 1988, the London *Sunday Telegraph* called Charles Dickens, "The Man Who Invented Christmas." *A Christmas Carol* played a significant role in that invention. Dickens published the story in December 1843. His sketches of Christmas draw from older ideals of traditions, warmth, family, food, and games that Victorian England had lost. Dickens' annual Christmas stories helped to reestablish those elements as an integral part of Christmas in popular imagination. Because the story contains many visual elements, *A Christmas Carol* has been adapted for stage and film productions multiple times, and the concept of "Scrooge" has become a staple among Christmas stories.

UNDERSTANDING LITERATURE:
Devices and Conventions

Like other books by Dickens, *A Christmas Carol* has an active **narrator**, although the narrator is not a character. The voice of the narrator is that of a storyteller. This perspective makes it easier for *A Christmas Carol* to present a simple and clear message to the reader.

Look at the following quotes from the opening scene of the story. What does each one tell you about the narrator? Is the narrator **limited** or **omniscient**? (Also, notice the use of **simile** in the third example.)

"Marley was dead, to begin with, there is no doubt whatever about that" (Dickens 30).

"Scrooge and he were partners for I don't know how many years."

"You will therefore permit me to repeat, emphatically, that Marley was as dead as a door-nail."

Stave 1: Marley's Ghost

Review Questions
1. How were Scrooge and Marley connected?
2. What word most accurately describes Scrooge's character?
3. Who came into the counting house on Christmas Eve?
4. What did Scrooge recommend be done with the poor?
5. What unusual sights and sounds did Scrooge notice when he came home that night?
6. Who visited Scrooge in his room?
7. Why did the ghost wear a chain?
8. What did the ghost tell Scrooge?

Thought Questions
1. Are you generally happier when you have money? If so, can wealth bring happiness?
2. What makes Christmas significant?
3. Is paid time off from employment for holidays natural? Is it reasonable?
4. Should you disregard business completely? Why or why not?

Stave 2: The First of the Three Spirits

Review Questions
1. Who visited Scrooge at one o'clock?
2. What was Scrooge's childhood like?
3. Was Mr. Fezziwig a good master? Why?
4. Why did Scrooge's fiancée leave him?

Thought Questions
1. Are people who did not receive love as children more or less likely to show it to others?
2. Do you agree with Scrooge, "There is nothing on which [the world] is so hard as poverty; and there is nothing it professes to condemn with such severity as the pursuit of wealth"?

Stave 3: The Second of the Three Spirits

Review Questions
1. When and how did the next spirit appear?
2. What did it represent?
3. What was wrong with Tiny Tim Cratchit?
4. What did the ghost tell Scrooge about Tiny Tim?
5. How did Scrooge's nephew feel about Scrooge?
6. How did the ghost change over the course of the night?
7. What two creatures clung to the spirit's robe?

Thought Questions
1. Is it more shameful to quarrel on Christmas Day than on any other day? Why or why not?
2. Who is hurt when shops are closed on the Seventh Day (Sunday)? Who receives benefit?
3. Why is ignorance more dangerous than want?

Stave 4: The Last of the Spirits

Review Questions
1. What final spirit approached Scrooge?
2. What event did the spirit and Scrooge hear everyone talking about?
3. Why did the charwoman, the laundress, and the undertaker's man meet at Old Joe's?
4. Did anyone feel emotion about the man's death? What kind of emotion did they feel?
5. What had happened to the Cratchits?
6. Who had died recently?

Thought Questions
1. Why do you think Scrooge was more afraid of this spirit than of any other?
2. Do individuals have the power to change their own future? To what extent?

Stave 5: The End of It

Review Questions
1. What day was it when Scrooge awoke?
2. What did Scrooge purchase for the Cratchits?
3. With whom did he spend Christmas?
4. Why did Scrooge arrive at work early the next day?
5. What did Scrooge do for the Cratchit family?

Thought Questions
1. Who do you think was hardest for Scrooge to face after his transformation?
2. Do you find Scrooge's transformation believable? Why or why not?
3. What does it mean to keep Christmas well?

WRITING REFINEMENT:
Applying Critical Lenses

Sometimes it is helpful to look at a book through a particular lens. The three lenses, or critical methods, mentioned in the introduction were feminist/multicultural, historical, and Marxist. Which of those three methods would be most suitable to *A Christmas Carol*? Start by asking yourself the following questions:

Does this book deal with different cultures or the treatment of minorities?

Does this book deal with a specific historical period?

Does this book deal with social classes or economics?

Based on your answers to these questions, choose a critical method that you think is relevant to *A Christmas Carol*. If you looked at *A Christmas Carol* through this lens, what incidents, characters, or situations might you choose to focus on? List 3-5 significant points.

A Passage to India
E. M. Forster

Edward Morgan Forster (1879-1970) was born in London. His earliest short stories were influenced by family trips around Europe. In 1915, during World War I, he went to Alexandria to serve in the Red Cross. Both before and after, he continued to travel extensively, including several trips to India. His writings frequently dealt with class differences, prejudice, and hypocrisy in the British Empire. *A Passage to India*, published in 1924, was his last novel, but he continued to write essays and to campaign against the censorship of literary works.

UNDERSTANDING LITERATURE:
Devices and Conventions

An author's style is often revealed in the type of content he or she chooses. Remember, most content can be defined as description (showing what something looks like), exposition (telling what is happening or explaining something), or dialogue (talking or thinking).

Look at this selection from *A Passage to India*.

> Astonishing even from the rise of the civil station, here the Marabar were gods to whom earth is a ghost. Kawa Dol was nearest. It shot up in a single slab, on whose summit one rock was poised—if a mass so great can be called one rock. Behind it, recumbent, were the hills that contained the other caves, isolated each from his neighbour by broad channels of the plain. The assemblage, ten in all, shifted a little as the train crept past them, as if observing its arrival. "I'd not have missed this for anything," said the girl, exaggerating her enthusiasm. (Forster 127)

First, rank the selection on the following scales:

	Slow		Average		Fast
Speed of reading	1	2	3	4	5

	Unclear		Average		Clear
Clarity of events	1	2	3	4	5

	Vague		Average		Vivid
Ability to visualize	1	2	3	4	5

Next, identify the parts of the selection that are description, exposition, and dialogue. If you want, you can use different colored pencils to underline or highlight each type of content. Approximately what percentage of the selection is description? Exposition? Dialogue? Which type of content do you think affects each scale you used to rank the selection? Find another passage from the book and mentally repeat this process, comparing the two selections.

Part I: The Mosque

Chapter 1

Review Questions
1. In what town or city and country did the novel take place?
2. What one feature near the city made it extraordinary, according to the locals?

Chapter 2

Review Questions
1. What had happened to Mahmoud Ali that morning in court?
2. What was the general consensus about the behavior of the English in India?
3. What family did Aziz have?
4. Who disrupted Aziz's reverie in the mosque?
5. How did she treat him differently than others like her did?

Thought Questions
1. The Indians debated whether it was possible to be friends with an Englishman. What features of colonial India made it necessary to ask this question?
2. What does it mean to "generalize from your disappointments"?

Chapter 3

Review Questions
1. Who was Adela Quested? Why had she come to India?
2. What was a "Bridge Party"?
3. How did Ronny react when he found out the young doctor his mother had met was a native?

4. What did Ronny ask Mrs. Moore not to discuss with Adela?

Thought Questions
1. What did Adela mean when she said she wanted to see the "real" India?
2. Why do you think the English judged the Indians so harshly? Were they justified in any way?

Chapter 4

Review Questions
1. What invitation did the Collector send out? Who received the invitation?

Thought Questions
1. Why did Ram Chand say the Indians would "make themselves cheap" by attending?
2. "Perhaps it is futile for men to initiate their own unity." Do you agree?

Chapter 5

Review Questions
1. What happened at the party? Was it a success? By whose standards?
2. Why did the educated Indians not matter to the Anglos?
3. According to Ronny, why were the English in India? What was not one of the reasons?

Chapter 6

Review Questions
1. Why had Aziz not gone to the party? What did he do instead?
2. How did he make an enemy of Panna Lal?

Thought Questions
1. Why did Aziz decide to make Panna Lal his enemy?
2. Were the Indians any more tolerant of those "below" them than the English were?

Chapter 7

Review Questions
1. Why was there a gulf between Mr. Fielding and the other Anglos?
2. What did Aziz give to Fielding?
3. Why did Aziz wear English dress?
4. What invitation did Aziz issue to the ladies?
5. How did the mood change when Ronny entered?

Thought Questions
1. "Ideas are fatal to caste." Why? Is the same thing true of any social hierarchy?
2. Why are Caucasians called "white" instead of a more descriptive term?
3. Is any racial term precisely accurate?

Chapter 8

Review Questions
1. What did Adela decide about the proposed engagement to Ronny?
2. What happened when Ronny and Adela rode in Nawab Bahadur's car?

3. What was Miss Derek doing in India?
4. How did Ronny sum up the character of Indians?
5. What did he assume about Aziz's missing collar stud? What was the real story?

Thought Questions
1. In India, did people of mixed race have an easier or more difficult time in society? Why?
2. Why did Adela change her mind about marrying Ronny? Did she have good reason?

Chapter 9

Review Questions
1. Why did Aziz want to go to Calcutta?
2. Who visited Aziz while he was ill?

Thought Questions
1. If English morals were declining, were the English justified in holding India?
2. What if their morals remained constant?
3. What are some of the differences between the way the English and the Indians communicated?

Chapter 10

Thought Questions
1. Forster tended to intersperse short, descriptive chapters between the dialogue and action. What purpose do these chapters serve?
2. Did the heat (the sun) become a character in the novel? If so, was it a hero or a villain?

Chapter 11

Review Questions
1. What did Aziz offer to show Fielding?
2. With what did Aziz say reform in India should begin?
3. Why did Fielding call Adela a "prig"? What did he mean?
4. Why was Fielding fearless about speaking his mind?

Thought Questions
1. Was Fielding's ability to "lay all his cards on the table" an individual trait or a cultural trait?
2. What are some of the reasons people choose to have children? Is it expected?

Part II: The Caves

Chapter 12

Review Questions
1. Describe the caves. What made them unique?

Chapter 13

Review Questions
1. Why did Aziz spend the night at the train station?
2. Why did Mr. Fielding and Professor Godbole not join the excursion?

Thought Questions
1. If you have ever visited another country, did the culture have a different understanding of time and punctuality? If so, what was it?
2. What are your culture's expectations for time and punctuality?

Chapter 14

Review Questions
1. What had Aziz hired to transport the group from the station to the caves?
2. Was Aziz knowledgeable about the caves?
3. Who was Aziz's hero? Why?
4. Why did Adela want some universal religion to exist in India?
5. Who went on to the higher caves on Kawa Dol?

Thought Questions
1. Is life dull? What makes it seem that way?
2. Why was it an honor to show hospitality, especially to foreigners?
3. Why was the echo in the caves so important (to Mrs. Moore)? What was its function?

Chapter 15

Review Questions
1. What did Adela realize about her upcoming marriage?
2. What offensive question did she ask Aziz as they climbed?

Chapter 16

Review Questions
1. Why did Adela and Aziz become separated?
2. Where did Miss Derek and Adela go when they left the group?
3. What happened when the party returned to Chandrapore?

Thought Questions
1. Compare these Urdu and English proverbs: 1) "If money goes, money comes; if money stays, death comes." 2) "A penny saved is a penny earned." What do these reveal about the cultures?

Chapter 17

Review Questions
1. What did the Collector tell Fielding about the arrest?
2. Why was Fielding's reaction distasteful to the Collector?
3. The breaking of what simple rule caused the incident, according to the Collector?

Thought Questions
1. "[Fielding] was still after facts, though the herd had decided on emotion." Were the

        rest of the English not interested in justice?
2. Can reason and emotion coexist?

Chapter 18

Review Questions
1. What was the precise accusation against Aziz? What was the evidence?
2. Why did Fielding want to be the one to question Adela about her memory of the events?
3. Was Fielding allowed to see Aziz? Why or why not?

Thought Questions
1. Why was frequenting a brothel shameful for an Indian but not for an Englishman?
2. What principle of justice was operating in this case? Innocent until proven guilty?

Chapter 19

Review Questions
1. Who was suggested to be Aziz's lawyer? Why?
2. What side did Fielding take?
3. Did Professor Godbole think Aziz was guilty or innocent? Who did he think was guilty?

Thought Questions
1. What are the pros and cons of taking sides (on religious questions, politics, social issues, etc.)?
2. Why do you think Professor Godbole seemed so unconcerned about Aziz?

Chapter 20

Review Questions
1. What was the effect of the incident on the character and temperament of the English?
2. At the club, what did the Collector advise the English to do?
3. What did Major Callendar say to bait Fielding?
4. What did Fielding want to say to the Collector?

Thought Questions
1. Why was it considered inappropriate to say Aziz's or Adela's name?
2. If "women and children" was an excuse to set aside sanity, what excuses are used today?
3. Was Fielding's approach at the club appropriate? Effective? Why or why not?

Chapter 21

Thought Questions
1. What errors of judgment did each side make in their evaluation of the situation?
2. Why do you think Forster set this (very short) chapter out as a separate chapter?

Chapter 22

Review Questions
1. Was any physical harm done to Adela?

2. Who was to preside over the trial?
3. Why did Adela begin to repeat Aziz's name?
4. Did Mrs. Moore have any evidence of Aziz's innocence?

Thought Questions
1. What effect had the attack had on Mrs. Moore?
2. Why do you think Adela changed her mind about Aziz's guilt?
3. Mrs. Moore said, "She has started the machinery; it will work to its end." What machinery?

Chapter 23

Review Questions
1. How did Mrs. Moore manage to leave India before the trial?

Thought Questions
1. Does everything (all words) amount to the same thing, as Mrs. Moore thought?
2. Why do you think the echo affected her so strongly?

Chapter 24

Review Questions
1. What signs of disquiet were displayed in the streets of the city before the trial?
2. Who represented the prosecution? What was his main argument?
3. What statement led Mahmoud Ali to leave the court?
4. At what point in her testimony did Adela falter?
5. What was the outcome of the trial?

Thought Questions
1. "Perhaps there is a grain of resentment in all chivalry." Do you agree?
2. Adela was forgotten in the fervor over her case. What does this tell you about that passion?
3. Did this trial represent justice? Try to identify some invalid claims on each side.

Chapter 25

Review Questions
1. Who took Adela away from the crowd?
2. Why did the mob want to attack the hospital?
3. How did Panna Lal stop them?

Chapter 26

Review Questions
1. What was Adela's explanation for her accusation?
2. Did Fielding believe in the supernatural?
3. Why did Ronny come to the College?
4. What news had he received about his mother?

Thought Questions
1. Do you think Adela understood the gravity of her accusations? Why or why not?
2. Why did Fielding say Adela "had become a real person" after the trial?

3. Discuss Hamidullah's behavior toward Adela and Ronny. Was it appropriate? Excusable?

Chapter 27

Review Questions
1. What did Fielding repeatedly ask Aziz to do?
2. Why was Aziz unwilling to comply?
3. What impossibility did Aziz propose as a compromise?

Thought Questions
1. Is it better to be unfair or materialistic (calculating) in your choice of friends? Why?
2. "People are not really dead until they are felt to be dead." Explain. Do you agree?

Chapter 28

Review Questions
1. What was Mrs. Moore's legacy in Chandrapore?
2. What did Ronny hope Adela would do?

Chapter 29

Review Questions
1. When he visited, what stance did the Lieutenant Governor take on the affair?
2. Why was Adela's letter of apology ineffective?
3. How did Fielding convince Aziz to renounce his claim for compensation from Adela?
4. What did Adela and Ronny decide to do?

Thought Questions
1. Do you think anyone actually followed Adela into the cave?

Chapter 30

Review Questions
1. What did Mr. Das ask Aziz to do?
2. What did Aziz want to leave Chandrapore in order to pursue?

Chapter 31

Review Questions
1. What caused the coolness between Fielding and Aziz?
2. Aziz suspected Fielding of what intentions for his trip to England?

Thought Questions
1. What does "traveling light" mean? What do you have to give up in order to do it?
2. Can rumors ruin a friendship if it is not already weak?

Chapter 32

Review Questions
1. What made the most impact on Fielding when he returned to the West?

Part III: The Temple
Chapter 33

Review Questions
1. What role did Professor Godbole serve in Mau?
2. What was Aziz's role?
3. Describe the Hindu ceremony of birth.

Thought Questions
1. How do conceptions of God fit into Forster's novel? How many different versions are there?
2. How is this Hindu ceremony related to the **plot** as a whole?

Chapter 34

Review Questions
1. Who arrived to visit Aziz in Mau? Why was Aziz unwilling to meet him?

Thought Questions
1. Is any religious group undivided? Why do you think sects and denominations arise?

Chapter 35

Review Questions
1. Who approached Aziz and his family at the Shrine of the Head?
2. Who was Fielding's wife?

Thought Questions
1. Why was Aziz so bitter toward Fielding? Did he blame Fielding for other Englishmen?
2. Was it inevitable that Aziz would become anti-English?

Chapter 36

Review Questions
1. What letters of Fielding's did Aziz read?
2. How did Aziz treat Ralph Moore when he met him alone at the guest house?
3. With what did Aziz and Ralph's boat collide?

Thought Questions
1. "Seeing India […] was only a form of ruling India." In what way? Discuss.
2. Why do you think Aziz loved Mrs. Moore so intensely?

Chapter 37

Review Questions
1. What did Aziz write to Adela?
2. When did Aziz say he and Fielding could be friends?

Thought Questions
1. Forster says of Aziz and Fielding, "Socially they had no meeting place." Was their friendship impossible? Why or why not?
2. Who is the hero/heroine of this book? Who is the villain?

WRITING REFINEMENT:
Analyzing Influences

This book focuses on the relationship between Britain and India in the early twentieth century. In order to write well about the book, you should know more about the social and cultural situation.

Using the Internet or a library, find three credible sources about British rule in India. Create a timeline of the main events beginning with India's colonization by the British and ending with India's independence. Include uprisings and the institution of new laws or acts. Then find out when Forster was in India and add that information to the timeline. How, if at all, does this change your perspective on the book?

Something Beautiful for God
Malcolm Muggeridge

Thomas Malcolm Muggeridge (1903-1990) was a British author and Christian apologist. As a young man, he taught school in India and Egypt before returning to England to take up a career in journalism. During World War II, he served in intelligence, but when the war was over, he returned to writing and editing. Muggeridge became a devout Christian as an adult, and his later writings reflect that change. In 1971, he wrote *Something Beautiful for God*, which chronicles the life of Mother Teresa. Mother Teresa (1910-1997) was born Agnes Gonxha Bojaxhiu in Macedonia. At the age of eighteen, she became a nun and was sent to India almost immediately. There, she founded her own order, "The Missionaries of Charity," and made her life's work homes for the poor and dying among India's untouchables—those no one else would help. In 1979, she was awarded the Nobel Peace Prize.

UNDERSTANDING LITERATURE:
Genre

Although biography is not fiction, it is still creative. It is impossible to include all of the details of an individual's life. The author chooses details with a view of the overall picture he or she wants to create. As you read *Something Beautiful for God*, pay attention to which periods in Mother Teresa's life are addressed briefly and which are dealt with extensively. What details does Muggeridge choose?

At Mother Teresa's request, Muggeridge wrote this book as a non-traditional biography. Think about the ways in which this book is NOT a normal biography. When you have finished the book, jot down a few thoughts about his purpose for writing. Is it to give information, or is it to persuade? Unlike autobiography, authors of biography bring their own perspective on their subject to their writing.

Chapter 1: Something Beautiful for God

Review Questions
1. Why did Mother Teresa not want Muggeridge to write this book as a biography?
2. How did Mother Teresa begin her ministry on the streets of Calcutta?
3. What, according to Mother Teresa, do the poor need most?
4. How did Muggeridge first meet Mother Teresa?
5. What miracle took place during the filming of the television documentary?
6. Why did Muggeridge hesitate to enter the church or take communion?

Thought Questions
1. What does it take to minister to someone? What does success in this field look like?
2. Can equality be achieved on earth? What is true equality?
3. "Either life is always and in all circumstances sacred, or intrinsically of no account; it is inconceivable that it should be in some cases the one, and in some the other." Discuss.
4. Muggeridge wrote in 1971 that miracles were unpopular. How are they viewed today?

Chapter 2: Mother Teresa's Way of Love

Review Questions
1. Did Mother Teresa think it was possible to love with the whole heart, mind, and soul?
2. On what two things does personal holiness depend?
3. What, according to Mother Teresa, is the biggest disease today?

Thought Questions
1. What does it mean to love God with your whole mind?
2. Does submission mean simply doing what you are told?
3. Is it necessary to suffer to serve God? Discuss.
4. Mother Teresa called hers a "high vocation." Do you agree?

Chapter 3: Mother Teresa Speaks

Review Questions
1. When did Mother Teresa's calling first come? Did she ever doubt it?
2. What was her second calling?
3. What did the Sisters do in a Home for the Dying?
4. What four vows did the Sisters take?
5. Did Mother Teresa promote individual or collective efforts?

Thought Questions
1. Why was it important that Mother Teresa waited for permission to leave the convent?
2. Would it be harder to enter a convent before or after experiencing the world? Why?
3. What makes Christian service different from social work?
4. Why is it harder to serve someone than to give money?

Chapter 4: A Door of Utterance

Review Questions

1. Did Mother Teresa believe in a different Jesus on the streets than at the altar?
2. Why is a "Jesus of history" a contradiction in terms?
3. According to Muggeridge, what circumstances could render God dead?
4. Did Muggeridge believe Mother Teresa was a saint?

Thought Questions
1. What does it mean to do "something beautiful for God"?
2. Is it possible to love your neighbor without loving God? Why or why not?
3. How do you answer the question, "Where is God?" when people suffer?

WRITING REFINEMENT:
Analyzing Influences

In order to understand why *Something Beautiful for God* is a non-traditional biography, imagine you are creating a traditional biography. This will give you greater insight into the choices a biographer makes. Using the library or the Internet, as well as the information in Muggeridge's book, create a brief timeline of Mother Teresa's life. Look up information about the social conditions in India when Mother Teresa began her work there, and include the status of her missions work since 1971, when Muggeridge's book was published.

Alice in Wonderland
Lewis Carroll

Charles Lutwidge Dodgson (1832-1898) began his career as a mathematician and logician teaching at Oxford University. A lover of beauty in many forms, Dodgson pursued photography as well as drama and poetry. In 1856, he began using the name "Lewis Carroll" to publish poetry and short fiction. In those pursuits, he was famous for word play and nonsense verse; his poem "Jabberwocky" is composed almost entirely of made-up words. In 1865, Carroll published the novel *Alice in Wonderland*, which was inspired in part by his friendship with the Liddell family and their daughter Alice. It was followed by a sequel, *Through the Looking Glass*, in 1872.

UNDERSTANDING LITERATURE:
Devices and Conventions

Alice in Wonderland is a children's fantasy novel. Alice questions basic assumptions about words and meaning, much as a child would. Carroll uses ambiguous words and **puns** to make a point. He also distorts rhymes and verses (familiar to his Victorian audiences) to give a very different meaning.

As Alice gets farther into Wonderland, she becomes more and more frustrated and uncomfortable. Carroll uses normal habits of conversation, things most people take for granted, to create this confusion. Look at the following passage. What makes it so difficult for the characters to carry on a normal conversation? What is the mood of the scene? Is it humorous or chaotic? What is the difference?

> "Take some more tea," the March Hare said to Alice, very earnestly. "I've had nothing yet," Alice replied in an offended tone: "so I ca'n't take more." "You mean you ca'n't take *less*," said the Hatter: "it's very easy to take *more* than nothing." "Nobody asked *your* opinion," said Alice. (Carroll 80)

Chapter 1: Down the Rabbit Hole

Review Questions
1. What disturbed Alice's sleepy afternoon?
2. What happened when Alice drank from the bottle that said "Drink Me"?

Thought Questions
1. Was Alice a logical person? Did she consider herself to be one?

Chapter 2: The Pool of Tears

Review Questions
1. What happened when Alice ate the cake that said "Eat Me"?
2. What effect did waving the fan have on Alice?

Thought Questions
1. Why do you think Carroll included the parts about Alice's mixed up knowledge? What purpose do they serve?

Chapter 3: A Caucus Race and a Long Tale

Review Questions
1. What was a caucus race (according to the Dodo)?
2. How did Alice offend the mouse and, later, the birds?

Thought Questions
1. What does "it" mean? How do you know? What gives words meaning?
2. What happens when you change the generally accepted meaning of a word?

Chapter 4: The Rabbit Sends in a Little Bill

Review Questions
1. Who was Mary Ann? Whom did the White Rabbit mistake for Mary Ann?
2. Why was Alice unable to get out of the White Rabbit's house?
3. How did she escape?

Thought Questions
1. Is it important that the lizard's name is Bill? What about the names of the other characters?
2. Why do you think Alice kept drinking and eating after such unusual things happened?
3. What effect does growing have on the way people view you? The way you view yourself?

Chapter 5: Advice from a Caterpillar

Review Questions
1. What advice did the Caterpillar give Alice?

Thought Questions
1. Is it possible to be "not yourself"? How? Discuss.

Chapter 6: Pig and Pepper

Review Questions
1. Who lived in the little house?
2. What became odd about the baby when Alice took it from the Duchess?
3. What was unusual about the Cheshire Cat?

Thought Questions
1. Do you agree with the Cheshire Cat when he said, "We're all mad here"? What did he mean?

Chapter 7: A Mad Tea-Party

Review Questions
1. Why was the Hatter on bad terms with Time?
2. Why was the tea table set for so many?

Thought Questions
1. Do people usually say what they mean?
2. Why do you think the tea party was so frustrating for Alice?

Chapter 8: The Queen's Croquet Ground

Review Questions
1. What kind of character was the Queen of Hearts?
2. What was different about the Queen's croquet game?
3. Who appeared to Alice in the middle of the game?

Chapter 9: The Mock Turtle's Story

Review Questions
1. What was the Mock Turtle?

Thought Questions
1. Does everything have a moral? Should it?

Chapter 10: The Lobster Quadrille

Thought Questions
1. Is it as funny to read mixed-up words as it is to hear them? Why or why not?
2. Is there a "porpoise" to this part of the story, or is it purely funny?

Chapter 11: Who Stole the Tarts?

Review Questions
1. Who was on trial? For what?
2. What did "suppressed" mean in reference to the guinea-pigs?
3. Who were the three witnesses?

Thought Questions
1. What do you think Carroll was saying, if anything, about the English justice system?
2. Do you think his parody would be an accurate portrayal of the American court system?

Chapter 12: Alice's Evidence

Review Questions
1. How was the matter of the tarts resolved?
2. What happened when all the cards attacked Alice?
3. What did Alice's sister dream?

Thought Questions
1. Why do you think Carroll added the serious tone in the last chapter? Does it seem out of place?
2. Is this just a funny book, or does it have a moral or a purpose? Why do you think so?

WRITING REFINEMENT: *Citing Sources*

When you are citing from a book, sometimes it is better to paraphrase, and sometimes it is better to quote directly. If you are dealing with a short quotation or something with very particular wording, it is best to quote directly. If, however, you only need the general sense of a passage or event, it is better to paraphrase—changing the words AND the sentence structure to make it your own.

In each of the following examples, look at the book to decide whether you would quote or paraphrase the scene in question. If you would paraphrase, practice doing it, and look back to make sure you have made it completely your own.

Use the Mad Hatter's tea party to show the way Carroll makes normal situations confusing.

Use the "Father William" poem to show how common verses are turned into mockery.

Use the courtroom scene to show that Alice has become more assertive by the end.

Use the Cheshire Cat's words to show that he is a helpful, not threatening, character.

Robinson Crusoe
Daniel Defoe

Daniel Defoe (1659/61-1731) was born in London. He was a Puritan in beliefs, and a prolific writer by trade. He began a career as a merchant, but he later became involved in politics, publishing pamphlets on political and religious affairs. Research in the nineteenth century confirmed rumors that Defoe had also been a government spy. Although most of his writing was journalistic in style, Defoe was one of the first to popularize the novel form in literature. His most popular work, *Robinson Crusoe*, was published in 1719. Defoe followed it quickly with a sequel: *Robinson Crusoe* and *The Farther Adventures of Robinson Crusoe* were published as a single book until the mid-nineteenth century, when publishers reverted to the practice of printing only the first part.

UNDERSTANDING LITERATURE:
Genre

Robinson Crusoe is considered one of the first English novels, a new convention in the eighteenth century. A novel has an extended, unified **plot** and deals with realistic situations and characters. Because of their length, novels could also include multiple sub-plots and a large cast of characters.

Robinson Crusoe was originally considered nonfiction because it was loosely based on a sailor's real experiences. As you read, see if you can identify the parts of the book that are clearly fiction. Look for "coincidences" that do not seem plausible. Also think about the characters. Do they seem realistic, or do they have qualities that seem to be artificially added? Think about the effect of depicting a work of fiction as nonfiction.

Since early editions of the novel do not include chapter divisions, these questions are based on general stages of the plot. Modern editions separate the book into chapters based on episodes in Crusoe's life.

Before the Island

Review Questions

1. What career did Robinson Crusoe want to enter? Why did his parents object?
2. How did Crusoe get to shore when his ship foundered?
3. In what role did Crusoe board the ship to Guinea?
4. What happened on his second voyage to Guinea?
5. How did Crusoe escape from the Moor? Who left with him?
6. How was Crusoe rescued? By whom?
7. Where and to what occupation did he settle temporarily?
8. What endeavor did Crusoe's fellow planters ask him to join?
9. What happened to the expedition? How many people survived?

Thought Questions

1. According to Father's logic, should the middle class today be the happiest people?
2. Why do you think people are "not ashamed to sin, and yet are ashamed to repent"?
3. Discuss Crusoe's treatment of Xury. Did Crusoe have the right to trade Xury to the captain?
4. Crusoe spent time as a slave. Do you think this had any effect on his view of slavery?

Alone on the Island

Review Questions

1. What animal life was present on the island?
2. How did Crusoe keep track of time?
3. What event led Crusoe to believe God was aiding him? Why did his faith quickly diminish?
4. Into what seasons did Crusoe separate the years on the island?
5. What land mass did Crusoe believe he sighted off the other side of the island?
6. Why was Crusoe's first attempt at building a boat ultimately useless?
7. What measure did Crusoe take to secure food for when his powder ran out?

Thought Questions

1. How much was the money on the ship worth to Crusoe? What does this tell you about the relative worth of money?
2. "All evils are to be considered with the good that is in them, and with what worse attends them." What does this mean to you?
3. Are people more likely to credit God with ordinary events or events that seemed impossible?
4. Why does God allow bad things to happen? Is this question inevitable?
5. Did Crusoe have any right of ownership over the island? Why did he assume that he did?
6. Is it difficult to believe that Crusoe "happened to have" so many skills and unknown resources?
7. Do you agree that Crusoe was "removed from all the wickedness of the world" on the island?

Crusoe's Companion

Review Questions

1. What surprise did Crusoe find in the sand of the shore near his boat?
2. How was the island used by others?

3. What defenses did Crusoe create?
4. What happened to the European ship that Crusoe heard approaching the island?
5. What did Crusoe dream?
6. How did his dream become reality?
7. What name did Crusoe give the man? Why?
8. Where had the man come from?
9. What religious beliefs did the man have?
10. Did Friday want to go home? What did he want Crusoe to do?

Thought Questions
1. Why is the fear of danger so much worse than danger itself?
2. Why does cannibalism seem so heinous? Is cannibalism murder?
3. Crusoe was able to justify cannibalism using an analogy of Christian warriors killing whole troops who had thrown down their swords. Discuss. Do you agree with his reasoning?
4. Did Crusoe have the right to treat Friday as a slave? Why or why not?
5. Are all men equal? Are they all the same? What is the difference?
6. Which American habits would members of another culture find strangest? Why?

Leaving the Island

Review Questions
1. Why did Friday and Crusoe attack the party of savages who came to the island?
2. How did Friday know the captive in the boat?
3. What did Crusoe plan to do with/for the sixteen white men on the mainland?
4. Who came to the island while the Spaniard and Friday's father were gone?
5. What bargain did Crusoe make with the mutineers?
6. What was done with the worst of the mutineers?

Thought Questions
1. Why was Crusoe so much more offended about the killing of a white man than of Caribbees?
2. Do you think Crusoe feared treachery more from the Spaniards or from the Caribbees? Why?
3. Was it natural for Crusoe to assign the white man to an overseeing role and the others to manual labor? Why do you think he did it?
4. In Crusoe's place, would you choose to leave the island or stay?
5. Was it unfair to the other Spaniards for Crusoe to leave without them?

Returning to England

Review Questions
1. What had happened to Crusoe's plantation in Brazil while he had been gone?
2. By what way did Crusoe return to England from Lisbon?
3. Why was Crusoe's company forced to stop in Pampeluna?
4. What dangers met the company and their guide in the mountains and forests?

Looking Back

Review Questions
1. What prevented Crusoe from settling down?
2. What had happened on the island in Crusoe's absence?

Thought Questions
1. Is it hard to believe that no one challenged Crusoe's right to ownership of the island?
2. How would you describe Crusoe's character? Is he likable? Admirable?

WRITING REFINEMENT:
Applying Critical Lenses

Which of the three critical methods (feminist/multicultural, historical, and Marxist) would be most suitable to *Robinson Crusoe*? Answer the following questions:

Does this book deal with different cultures or the treatment of minorities?

Does this book deal with a specific historical period?

Does this book deal with social classes or economics?

Based on your answers to these questions, choose a critical method that you think is relevant to *Robinson Crusoe*. If you looked at *Robinson Crusoe* through this lens, what incidents, characters, or situations might you choose to focus on? List 3-5 significant points.

Selections from *Father Brown*

G. K. Chesterton

Gilbert Keith Chesterton (1874-1936) began his education in art school, and his first writings were in the genre of art criticism, but his scholarly and professional interests were not limited to one field. His first book was a collection of poetry, released in 1900. He went on to write extensively as a journalist; in addition, he wrote short stories, plays, essays, and novels, producing over a hundred books and collections of shorter works. A Catholic and a thinker as well as a writer, his work deals with contemporary philosophy, ethics, and questions of faith. In 1911, Chesterton created the fictional priest-detective Father Brown for a collection of short stories called *The Innocence of Father Brown*. Father Brown was featured in a total of five collections of short stories, continuing in *The Wisdom of Father Brown* (1914), *The Incredulity of Father Brown* (1926), *The Secret of Father Brown* (1927), and *The Scandal of Father Brown* (1935). The Father Brown stories combine a strong sense of humor with insightful commentary on the nature of man.

UNDERSTANDING LITERATURE:
Devices and Conventions

Chesterton's Father Brown stories fit into the genre of mystery or detective short stories. However, Father Brown, like Chesterton himself, was deeply interested in human nature, and the stories reflect that philosophical leaning. This is an instance in which one genre is used as a vehicle for a secondary purpose.

As you read the stories, ask yourself whether their main purpose is to entertain and intrigue or to teach. It may be a combination of both. Are they most effective as entertainment or as philosophy? If you had to guess, which do you think Chesterton intended? Keep in mind that teaching is sometimes best when it is a secondary rather than primary feature.

If you can, read a variety of Father Brown stories to get a sense of Father Brown's detective methods, the type of cases and solutions he encounters, and Chesterton's writing style. These questions are derived from stories in all five Father Brown collections. Most questions should apply to any Father Brown story.

Review Questions

1. How is Father Brown described? Is he ordinary or unique in appearance?
2. What is Father Brown's typical method of detecting (his *modus operandi*)?
3. What great criminal, who later became Father Brown's friend, appears in several stories?
4. Where does Father Brown get his information about criminal minds and methods?
5. What is Father Brown's most common objective: to catch criminals, prevent crimes, solve mysteries, convert criminals, or something else?

Thought Questions

1. What makes a great detective?
2. Compare Father Brown to Sherlock Holmes, Brother Cadfael, and other legendary detectives. How are they alike? How are they different?
3. Who do you think is the best detective? What criteria are you using to make that decision?
4. Does Father Brown's role as a priest affect his abilities as a detective?
5. Do you think the reader has a fair chance to solve the mysteries? Re-read one of the stories with the solution in mind. Could you reach that explanation from the clues given?
6. Why did Father Brown believe it was "bad theology" to attack reason?
7. Why are priests and other members of the clergy assumed to be ignorant of this world?
8. In "The Blue Cross," Father Brown said, "A man who does next to nothing but hear men's real sins is not likely to be wholly unaware of human evil." Is it possible to hear so much evil without being tainted by it?
9. If both are equally clever, what is the main difference between a criminal and a detective?

WRITING REFINEMENT:
Applying Critical Lenses

Comparing multiple works of literature allows you to notice the subtleties that set one author's style apart from another's. The Father Brown stories by Chesterton are among a long tradition of detective stories. Take a minute to list 3-5 identifying characteristics of Chesterton's detective and his writing style.

Next, look at the two quotes below. Both are the final comments of a detective after solving a mystery. One of them is from a Father Brown mystery. The other is from a Sherlock Holmes mystery by Sir. Arthur Conan Doyle. **Without looking** at the answer at the bottom of the page, decide which one comes from *Father Brown*. How do you know?

1. "'Well, it is a great responsibility that I take upon myself, but I have given Hopkins an excellent hint, and if he can't avail himself of it I can do no more. See here, Captain Crocker, we'll do this in due form of law. You are the prisoner [...] I am the judge. Now, gentleman of the jury, you have heard the evidence. Do you find the prisoner guilty or not guilty?'"[3]

2. "'Well, that is the whole of this simple village idyll, I think. But you will admit I kept my promise; I have shown you something in the village considerably more creepy than a corpse; even a corpse stuffed with poison. The black coat of a parson stuffed with a blackmailer is at least worth noticing and my live man is much deadlier than your dead one.'"[4]

---

[3] "The Adventure of the Abbey Grange" by Doyle.
[4] "The Vampire of the Village" by Chesterton.

A Morbid Taste for Bones
Ellis Peters

Edith Mary Pargeter (1913-1995) was an English writer of Welsh heritage. As a young woman, she worked as a chemist's assistant and gained knowledge of medicine that featured prominently in some of her later detective novels. She published her first novel in 1936. During World War II, Pargeter served as an administrator in the Women's Royal Naval Service, but she continued to write and publish. Although she is best known for her murder mysteries, she did not publish the first of this genre until 1951. When she started to write crime fiction, she adopted the pen name Ellis Peters to keep this work separate from her earlier writing. One of her most famous characters is the Welsh monk and detective Brother Cadfael, who appeared in twenty novels and a collection of short stories. *A Morbid Taste for Bones*, the first book featuring Brother Cadfael, was published in 1977.

UNDERSTANDING LITERATURE:
Genre

The content of a detective novel is carefully designed to give the reader a sense of expectation. Every detail is chosen with the intent to tantalize and, subtly, to inform. Characters are introduced as potential suspects, with certain characteristics that will affect their later behavior.

Look at the following list of characters from *A Morbid Taste for Bones*. As you read, notice the place where each character is introduced. Jot down the particular details that are given in relation to that character. Note your impression of the character.

Brother Cadfael –

Brother John –

Brother Columbanus –

Brother Jerome –

Prior Robert –

Father Huw –

Lord Rhisiart –

Sioned –

Peredur –

Annest –

Engelard –

When you have finished the book, compare the introduction of the character to his or her ultimate role in the **plot**. Why did Peters choose the particular details she did? Was your first impression misleading or accurate? If it was misleading, how did Peters mislead you—and why?

Chapter 1

Review Questions
  1. What was Brother Cadfael's special gift?
  2. What had he done before becoming a monk?
  3. What awakened Cadfael from his dream?
  4. What method of healing did Brother Jerome suggest the next morning?
  5. Who was Winifred?
  6. Did the well heal Columbanus?
  7. On what grounds did Cadfael and Brother John join the expedition to Wales?

Thought Questions
  1. Would it take more dedication to become a monk/nun when you were old or young? Why?
  2. Is it impossible to do things for both God's and man's glory?

Chapter 2

Review Questions
  1. Why did Father Huw resist the Shrewsbury brothers' mission?
  2. What distracted Brother Cadfael and Brother John during the conversation with Father Huw?
  3. What meeting did Cadfael observe outside the town?

Thought Questions
  1. Guests were "sacrosanct" in this culture. How has that changed? Why has it changed?
  2. Does "leading and coaxing [pay] better than driving"? Why or why not?

Chapter 3

Review Questions
  1. Who was Rhisiart? Why was he important?
  2. Who was his daughter? What stood in the way of her happy marriage?
  3. Who argued against Prior Robert at the meeting? What was the outcome?

4. What was Prior Robert's "disastrous miscalculation" in his attempt to persuade Rhisiart?

Thought Questions
1. Does God, as Brother Cadfael suggested, require "a little help from men"? Discuss.
2. Women and villeins had no part in the assembly. Should you judge a culture's customs?
3. Why is money an "aberration in human relations"? Is it?

Chapter 4

Review Questions
1. What did Father Huw propose as a means of achieving reconciliation? Did Rhisiart agree?
2. Where did Columbanus and Jerome go while Prior Robert waited for Rhisiart?
3. Why did the meeting not take place as planned?
4. What happened to Rhisiart?

Chapter 5

Review Questions
1. What could Rhisiart tell the gathered people?
2. To whom did the arrow belong?
3. How did Engelard escape the gathering?

Thought Questions
1. Is it hypocritical to have a blood feud among Christians? Why or why not?
2. Prior Robert said, "Avenging saints may make use of earthly instruments," and Brother Cadfael responded, "The instrument would still be a murderer." Do you agree?

Chapter 6

Review Questions
1. What did Columbanus confess at chapter?
2. What news did Father Huw bring?
3. How did Peredur react when Brother Cadfael delivered Sioned's message?
4. What "miracle" did Prior Robert perform at Saint Winifred's grave?
5. What had killed Rhisiart?

Thought Questions
1. What do you think of Brother Cadfael's advice, "Meet every man as you find him, for we're all made the same under habit or robe or rags"?

Chapter 7

Review Questions
1. What trial of guilt did all the villagers believe?
2. How did Brother Cadfael use it?
3. Did Rhisiart bleed when Jerome touched him?
4. Why had Brother John taken the cowl?
5. What happened to Columbanus while he and Cadfael kept watch?

Thought Questions
1. Was it ethical for Brother Cadfael to alter the conversation when he translated for Prior Robert and the prince's bailiff? Why or why not?

Chapter 8

Review Questions
1. What did Columbanus say when he awoke?
2. Who actually uncovered Winifred's skeleton?
3. What happened when Peredur tried to touch Rhisiart?
4. What did Peredur confess?

Thought Questions
1. Why did Peredur still want to place Sioned's cross on her father before leaving?

Chapter 9

Review Questions
1. What did Brother Cadfael hint could be done for Brother John?
2. What was wrong with Peredur's mother?
3. When Cadfael found the bottle of poppy syrup, what did he realize?
4. Why did the bailiff decide to take Brother John that morning?
5. What did Annest tell Cadfael that allowed him to plan one final trap?
6. What did Prior Robert and the bailiff find at Rhisiart's when they went to collect Brother John?

Thought Questions
1. Do you agree with Brother Cadfael that men and women have the same basic natures?

Chapter 10

Review Questions
1. What did Brother Columbanus dream?
2. What did he confess?
3. How did Columbanus discover the trap?
4. What happened when Columbanus tried to escape?
5. How did Brother Cadfael recommend explaining the night's events?

Thought Questions
1. Was Brother Cadfael right to cover up what really happened, given the circumstances?
2. Does the end justify the means?

Chapter 11

Review Questions
1. What did Prior Robert find at the chapel?
2. How did Brother Cadfael explain the weight of the reliquary?

Thought Questions
1. "Miracles have nothing to do with reason […] If they made sense, they would not be miracles." Do you agree?

Chapter 12

Review Questions
1. What news did Bened bring about Winifred's grave?

Thought Questions
1. Were you able to figure out the mystery before it was revealed?
2. What clues did Peters leave in the early parts of the book?

WRITING REFINEMENT:
Comparing Ideas

Both of the last two works are detective or crime stories, and both heroes are religious. However, *Brother Cadfael* is a novel and the Father Brown mysteries are short stories. Consider the innate differences between Brother Cadfael and Father Brown. How are their methods of solving crimes different? How are Peters' and Chesterton's storytelling methods different?

Novels and short stories, because of their lengths, must be handled differently. Although both Peters' and Chesterton's detectives have a lot in common, the medium of the works you have read makes them inherently different. Think about what the author has to do for each medium to be successful, and what the limitations and advantages are for each medium. Choose one Father Brown story, and answer the following questions:

- How many significant characters are in *A Morbid Taste for Bones*?
- How many significant characters are in the Father Brown story?
- What is the **climax** of *A Morbid Taste for Bones*?
- What is the climax of the Father Brown story?
- Does anything happen after the climax in *A Morbid Taste for Bones*?
- Does anything happen after the climax in the Father Brown story?

Based on your answers, develop 3-5 sentences arguing that either the short story form or the novel form is more effective for detective stories like those written by Peters and Chesterton.

Out of the Silent Planet
C. S. Lewis

Clive Staples Lewis (1898-1963) was born in Ireland. After serving in the British army during World War I, he became a professor of literature at Oxford, where he had previously attended college, and later at Cambridge. The son of Christian parents, Lewis became an atheist as a young man, but he later re-considered Christianity and was converted in 1931, becoming one of the great Christian writers and speakers of the twentieth century. In addition to his nonfiction writings, Lewis is famous for the seven children's fantasy novels in the *Chronicles of Narnia*, as well as a trilogy of science fiction novels. *Out of the Silent Planet*, published in 1938, is the first in the Space Trilogy. It was followed by *Perelandra* (1943) and *That Hideous Strength* (1945).

UNDERSTANDING LITERATURE:
Genre

Many of the principles of science fiction and fantasy writing are the same. In both instances, the author has to create a world that is different enough to seem new but familiar enough to be understandable. What classifies *Out of the Silent Planet* as science fiction is the fact that 1) it is set in this universe, and 2) Lewis offers some material explanation for the surrealistic elements in the novel. The main characters travel through space using what are presumed to be scientific methods. By contrast, in a fantasy novel, supernatural elements are accepted as a natural part of the alternate reality in which they exist.

Because both science fiction and fantasy depend on the author to create a world that readers can accept as believable, the content of these novels has to be adjusted accordingly, often to include more description and explanation than another type of novel might require. Look at chapter 7 of *Out of the Silent Planet*, in which the travelers land on the new planet. After re-reading the chapter, give an estimate for what percentage of the chapter consists of description, and what percentage is exposition or dialogue. Compare this to the first chapter of the book, in which the travelers are on Earth, and consider what other authors take for granted when they write about real places and settings.

Chapter 1

Review Questions
   1. Where was the Pedestrian going? Who was he?
   2. Who lived at The Rise?
   3. What had happened to the woman's son?

Chapter 2

Review Questions
   1. Why had Ransom chosen to take a walking tour?
   2. What happened to Ransom while Devine was speaking?

Thought Questions
   1. Why did using Ransom for testing bother Weston, when using Harry did not?
   2. Is it ever ethical to use humans for lab testing? If not, why not?

Chapter 3

Review Questions
   1. What was unusual about the room in which Ransom awoke?
   2. What did the size and brightness of the moon tell Ransom about his surroundings?

Thought Questions
   1. What does it take for your perspective on something ordinary to change?
   2. Are perceptions ever flawed? How do you find out?

Chapter 4

Review Questions
   1. Where were Weston and Devine taking Ransom?
   2. What was the place called? Who called it that?
   3. Why were directions so strange on the ship?

Thought Questions
   1. Did Ransom lose his rights because he snuck into Weston's yard? Why or why not?
   2. Weston said, "Small claims must give way to great." Do you agree?

Chapter 5

Review Questions
   1. What did Devine hope to get out of the adventure?
   2. What had "Space" previously meant to Ransom? How did that change?
   3. What conversation did Ransom overhear? Why did it make him nervous?

Thought Questions
1. Does space make humans seem insignificant, or just small? Is that a good thing?
2. Why is "otherness" so frightening?

Chapter 6

Review Questions
1. How did the travelers know they were approaching land?

Thought Questions
1. Ransom speculated about the "real void" and the "real light." What do you think they are?

Chapter 7

Review Questions
1. Describe the new planet.
2. Who had built the hut on the water's edge?
3. What kind of creatures approached the three men?
4. How did Ransom escape?

Chapter 8

Review Questions
1. How did Ransom stay warm at night?

Thought Questions
1. Do humans have a "survival instinct"? Do people value life, or just their own life?
2. Why do you think Ransom's self love was so much stronger when he was alone?

Chapter 9

Review Questions
1. Why was Ransom glad to see the giraffe-like animals?
2. What was the "perpendicular theme" on Malacandra?
3. What did Ransom meet coming out of the water?
4. What reassured Ransom as to the creature's intentions?

Thought Questions
1. "The love of knowledge is a kind of madness," Ransom said. What do you think he meant?
2. How do you learn to communicate with someone if neither person knows the other's language?
3. Why was the creature disgusting if Ransom thought of it as a man, but delightful if he thought of it as an animal?

Chapter 10

Review Questions
1. What did the *hross* invite Ransom to do?
2. What were the differences between the *harandra* and the *handramit*?
3. Where did the *hrossa* live? The *sorns*?

Chapter 11

Review Questions
1. What is the difference between being in a new place and going to a new place?
2. Describe the *hrossa* culture.
3. What did the *hrossa* call Earth? Why?
4. Was there a ruling class on Malacandra?

Thought Questions
1. How does the religion of the *hrossa* compare to Christianity?

Chapter 12

Review Questions
1. What was the *hrossa* understanding of love and relationships?
2. What were the *eldila*?

Thought Questions
1. One of the *hross* said, "A pleasure is fully grown only when it is remembered." Do you agree?
2. Does danger make you appreciate life more fully? Why?

Chapter 13

Review Questions
1. What was Ransom's role in the hunt for the *hnakra*?
2. What message did the *eldil* give?
3. What happen to Hyoi?
4. Where did Whin send Ransom?

Chapter 14

Review Questions
1. What happened to the air after Ransom reached a certain height?
2. What did Ransom find in the cavern at the top of the mountains?

Chapter 15

Review Questions
1. How did the creature know Ransom was from Thulcandra?
2. Who was Augray?
3. What was the *sorns'* occupation?
4. How did Augray show Ransom Earth?

Thought Questions
1. Discuss Augray's explanation of the *eldil* and of Oyarsa. Do you understand it? Is it logical?
2. "The bleakest moment in all his travels" was when Ransom found out Earth was the same place as Thulcandra. Why?

Chapter 16

Thought Questions
1. Is it valuable to have events and histories written down? Why?
2. Why is it necessary to have rulers? Is it? How does a democracy fit into this idea?

Chapter 17

Review Questions
1. What was Meldilorn like?
2. What was depicted on the most unusual stone at the center of the island?
3. Which planet was Malacandra?
4. What did the *pfifltrigg* want Ransom to do?
5. Why did all the Malacandrians speak the *hrossa's* language?

Chapter 18

Review Questions
1. What did Oyarsa tell Ransom about his trip from Earth?
2. What questions had Oyarsa wanted to ask Ransom or another human?
3. Who arrived from the ferry in the middle of Ransom's audience with Oyarsa?

Thought Questions
1. How does Oyarsa's account of Earth's history compare to the Bible's account?
2. Are there elements of this book that could be allegorical? Why or why not?

Chapter 19

Review Questions
1. What was Weston's approach to dealing with Oyarsa?
2. What did Oyarsa prescribe to make Weston more sensible?

Chapter 20

Review Questions
1. What did Devine propose?
2. What justification did Weston give for his actions?
3. Why did Oyarsa say Weston was bent, but Devine was broken?
4. Why was Devine opposed to leaving Malacandra?
5. What did Oyarsa decide regarding the three men's fate?

Thought Questions
1. How accurate was Ransom's translation for Weston?
2. Did he change the message's meaning? Its tone?
3. Weston said, "Life is greater than any system of morality." What is wrong with this argument?
4. On what are systems of morality built?
5. What did Weston love?

Chapter 21

Review Questions
1. What charge did Oyarsa lay on Ransom?
2. What was different/worse about the return journey? Why?
3. What complicated the final approach to Earth?

Thought Questions
1. This chapter opens, "I am not going to record [the conversation between Ransom and Oyarsa]." Why do you think Lewis introduced a personal **narrator** at this point? What is the effect?
2. Is there a link between history and mythology? If so, what?

Chapter 22

Review Questions
1. Why was this book truly written?
2. Who was "I"? How was he connected to Ransom?

Thought Questions
1. Is fiction all false?
2. Do you think Weston or Ransom were based on real people? Support your answer.

Postscript

1. What is the effect of this addition? Does it make the contents seem more real?
2. Why do you think Lewis used his own name to represent the narrator ("I")?

WRITING REFINEMENT: *Analyzing Influences*

Out of the Silent Planet is as much a book about philosophy as it is a book about another planet. Each character has a certain perspective on ethics, science, and humanity. Although popular debates about these topics were based on different issues when Lewis wrote the book, similar questions arise today.

Take a minute to write down some of the ethical and moral dilemmas that modern scientists and intellectuals are debating. What position would the characters in Lewis's novel take on each of these questions? What position do you think Lewis would take? If possible, research the dilemmas that were prevalent in Lewis's day. Which ones do you think this book addresses?

Keep this information in mind as you analyze the characters' moral perspectives and decisions.

The Hobbit
J. R. R. Tolkien

John Ronald Reuel Tolkien (1892-1973) was born in South Africa but moved to England when he was young. After serving in the British army during World War I, he returned to take up scholarly work as a philologist and professor of literature. Tolkien had already begun to develop a system of languages based on Finnish, and with them, a fantasy world influenced by Norse sagas and Old English poetry. Tolkien was also a devout Catholic, and elements of his faith can be seen in his founding myths, which were published posthumously as the *Book of Lost Tales*. Tolkien continued to develop his mythology and languages, but *The Hobbit*, his first complete novel set in Middle Earth, originated from stories that Tolkien told his children. *The Hobbit* was published in 1937, and its success led to the development of the sequel, *The Lord of the Rings* trilogy, which was published between 1954 and 1955 as *The Fellowship of the Ring*, *The Two Towers*, and *The Return of the King*.

UNDERSTANDING LITERATURE:
Genre

Tolkien's fantasy world, Middle Earth, is well known in part because it was so thoroughly crafted. Tolkien developed languages for each culture; he created history, mythology, and literature; he included maps and linguistic guides with the books; he also added the quirks and oddities of culture. As a result, readers of the novels have access to an array of information comparable to that recorded by historians about real civilizations.

The novel is written deliberately to give a sense of depth and longevity. For each of these passages, see if you can identify the techniques that bring the fantasy realm of Middle Earth to life and make it seem like a real place with a real history.

1. "If you have ever seen a dragon in a pinch, you will realize that this was only poetical exaggeration applied to any hobbit, even to Old Took's great-granduncle Bullroarer" (Tolkien 30).

2. "'These are not troll-make. They are old swords, very old swords of the High Elves of the West, my kin. They were made in Gondolin for the Goblin-wars.

They must have come from a dragon's hoard or goblin plunder, for dragons and goblins destroyed that city many ages ago.[…] This, Gandalf, was Glamdring, Foe-hammer that the king of Gondolin once wore'" (Tolkien 61).

Chapter 1: An Unexpected Party

Review Questions
 1. Which family of hobbits was known for occasionally having adventures?
 2. What was Gandalf's reputation in the Shire?
 3. Who came to Bilbo's house for tea?
 4. What role did they want Bilbo to play in their upcoming adventure?

Thought Questions
 1. Do greetings have actual meaning, or are they simply rituals?
 2. What is the difference between a warrior and a hero? Is there one?

Chapter 2: Roast Mutton

Review Questions
 1. Whose campfire did the company see when they stopped for the night?
 2. What did Bilbo attempt to do? How did he get caught?
 3. How did Gandalf rescue the dwarves?
 4. What did Gandalf and Thorin take from the trolls' lair?

Thought Questions
 1. Why do you think Bilbo joined the dwarves' company: peer pressure or desire for adventure?

Chapter 3: A Short Rest

Review Questions
 1. What was Rivendell?
 2. Who had made the swords that Gandalf and Thorin had taken? What were their names?
 3. What did the moon letters on the map reveal?

Thought Questions
 1. If you have seen the *Lord of the Rings* films, how are elves portrayed differently in this book?
 2. Why do pleasant things not make a good tale but gruesome things do? Is this still true?

Chapter 4: Over Hill and Under Hill

Review Questions
 1. Where did the company go to escape the thunderstorm?
 2. What happened to them during the night?
 3. What did the goblins discover that made them hate Thorin worse than before?
 4. How did the company escape?
 5. Why was Bilbo left behind?

Thought Questions
1. Tolkien repeatedly said Bilbo wished to go home. What does this tell you about Bilbo?
2. Why do you think the swords in *The Hobbit* were given names/personalities? Have you seen this practice in any other books? How do those books compare to *The Hobbit*?

Chapter 5: Riddles in the Dark

Review Questions
1. What did Bilbo find on the floor of the tunnel?
2. Whom did Bilbo meet at the edge of the underground lake?
3. What contest did the creature propose? How did Bilbo win?
4. Why did the creature go back to his island? What was he looking for?
5. How did Bilbo escape the caves?

Thought Questions
1. Was Bilbo's a fair victory in the game? Why or why not?
2. What is your first impression of Gollum? Do you pity him? Do you think Bilbo did?
3. Why did Bilbo not kill Gollum? Was this choice wise?

Chapter 6: Out of the Frying-Pan into the Fire

Review Questions
1. Where did the company go to hide from the wolves?
2. Why did the Lord of the Eagles know Gandalf?

Thought Questions
1. Are certain types of animals naturally "good" and "evil"?
2. Why are they portrayed that way in books and films?
3. The characters in *The Hobbit* are often rescued by some unforeseen ally. Why?

Chapter 7: Queer Lodgings

Review Questions
1. To whose home did Gandalf guide the dwarves?
2. Why did Gandalf instruct the dwarves to enter two by two and at intervals?
3. What did Beorn tell the dwarves not to do in Mirkwood?
4. Where did Gandalf leave the company?

Thought Questions
1. Each culture in *The Hobbit* has standards of polite conduct. What are American standards?

Chapter 8: Flies and Spiders

Review Questions
1. What happened to Bombur when he fell in the black stream?
2. Why did the dwarves leave the path?
3. What did Bilbo name his sword? After what event did he name it?
4. What had happened to Thorin?

Thought Questions
1. Bilbo acted bravely in his fight with the spiders. At what point do you think he became brave?
2. Why were the elves and dwarves enemies?
3. Is it natural for cultures to clash? If so, why?

Chapter 9: Barrels Out of Bond

Review Questions
1. How did Bilbo rescue the dwarves from the Elvenking's palace?
2. What had he forgotten in his grand escape plans?

Thought Questions
1. In the **conflict** between dwarves and elves, did one side have the right to be angry? Which one?
2. Was Bilbo skilled or just lucky in engineering the escape?

Chapter 10: A Warm Welcome

Review Questions
1. What was unusual about the architecture of Lake-town?
2. How were the dwarves treated in Lake-town?

Thought Questions
1. What role did public opinion play in the Master's decision to welcome the dwarves?

Chapter 11: On the Doorstep

Review Questions
1. Why were the dwarves' tools incapable of opening the secret door?
2. How did the dwarves finally get the door open?

Thought Questions
1. Did the dwarves always get someone else to get them out of trouble? Are there exceptions?

Chapter 12: Inside Information

Review Questions
1. What did Bilbo take from the dragon's hoard? How did the dragon respond?
2. What was the way to talk to dragons?
3. What advice did Smaug give Bilbo?
4. Where was Smaug's weak spot?
5. What did the dwarves promise Bilbo about the treasure?
6. What was the greatest treasure in the hoard?
7. What did Smaug do at night after talking to Bilbo?

Thought Questions
1. By this point, how has Bilbo changed from the beginning of the book?
2. Why is the most difficult part of a plan often forgotten?

Chapter 13: Not at Home

Review Questions
1. How did the company get out of the tunnel?
2. What did Bilbo find when he was alone in the dragon's hall?
3. What did Thorin give Bilbo?

Chapter 14: Fire and Water

Review Questions
1. Where did Smaug go after he left the mountain?
2. Who led the defense against the dragon?
3. How was Smaug defeated?
4. Whom did the Lake-men blame for the destruction of their town?
5. Why did the Elvenking and Bard march toward the mountain?

Chapter 15: The Gathering of the Clouds

Review Questions
1. How did the dwarves get news from the thrush? What was his news?
2. What did the dwarves decide to do?
3. What did the Elvenking and Bard demand? On what grounds?

Thought Questions
1. Thorin was willing to exchange peace for gold. Have any real leaders shared this mentality?
2. Who had a right to the treasure?
3. Does gold (money) have the same power over people's hearts today?

Chapter 16: A Thief in the Night

Review Questions
1. What did Bilbo do with the Arkenstone?
2. Who congratulated him as he left the camp of the elves and men?

Thought Questions
1. Would you classify Bilbo as a traitor, a burglar, a diplomat, or something else? Why?
2. Did Bilbo have a right to the Arkenstone?

Chapter 17: The Clouds Burst

Review Questions
1. What bargain did Bard offer Thorin?
2. Who prevented Thorin from harming Bilbo?
3. Who arrived to support Thorin?
4. What stopped the battle between the elves, men, and dwarves?
5. What did Bilbo do during the battle?

Thought Questions
1. Why are people most proud of memories that were unpleasant while they were happening?

Chapter 18: The Return Journey

Review Questions
1. What was Thorin's last message to Bilbo?
2. Who had finally won the battle? How?
3. What treasure did Bilbo take with him when he left?

Chapter 19: The Last Stage

Review Questions
1. What had Gandalf done while he was apart from the rest?
2. What did Bilbo find when he got home?

Thought Questions
1. The journey home after an adventure can be easy to forget. Why do you think Tolkien included this part instead of ending with triumph?
2. Did Bilbo manage his adventures and escape by sheer luck?
3. What larger things did his actions affect?
4. Was Bilbo a hero? Compare his characteristics to someone like Beowulf.

WRITING REFINEMENT: *Comparing Ideas*

This is another good opportunity to think about comparing multiple works. *The Hobbit* is a fantasy, and *Out of the Silent Planet* is a science fiction novel. Both books, however, deal with the development of an unfamiliar world.

Look at the way each author crafted the history and culture of the new world: Malacandra and Middle Earth. What are some similarities between the two worlds? What are some differences? Can you see Christian undertones in both?

What would you have to change to make *The Hobbit* a science fiction novel? What would you have to change to make *Out of the Silent Planet* a purely fantasy novel? Would either one be as effective in this format? One key difference between science fiction and fantasy is that science fiction allows for interaction between the "real world" and the fantastical world, although not all science fiction uses this technique. Think about the benefits and disadvantages of using this device, as Lewis did.

The Screwtape Letters
C. S. Lewis

C.S. Lewis wrote *The Screwtape Letters* as a series of letters written between a demon and his underling, in which the senior demon, Screwtape, gives his young protégé, Wormwood, advice on the best methods for tempting humans. *The Screwtape Letters*, which would become one of Lewis's most popular works of fiction for adults, was published in *The Guardian*, a Christian newspaper in London, in installments from May to December, 1941. The book was published in full in 1942.

UNDERSTANDING LITERATURE:
Genre

This novel is written in what is known as epistolary form. An epistolary novel is composed solely of letters written by the characters. The epistolary form uses **first person** narration, which shows the writer's personality. Although in this case the return letters from Wormwood are not included, Screwtape **alludes** to them in his letters, giving readers suggestions about their style and content.

Think for a minute about what is different when an author uses letters to tell a story. How do you read this type of book differently? What does the author have to do in order to convincingly tell the story from the letter writer's perspective?

As you read, try to identify 3-5 characteristics of Screwtape's writing style. How does he refer to himself? To Wormwood? What words does he use repeatedly? Does he use a particular sentence structure? Verb tense? Also, consider how Screwtape's voice changes over the course of the book.

Please note: The review questions are based on Screwtape's perspective. Their purpose is to make sure you have a good grasp of what is being said in each letter. The thought questions, however, are to be answered from your own perspective.

Letter 1

Review Questions
1. Who was "the Enemy"?
2. Who/what were Screwtape and Wormwood?
3. What was their relationship to each other?
4. Why did Screwtape say arguments are not the way to keep people from the Enemy?

Thought Questions
1. What do you call "real life"? Is it just a distraction?
2. Is reason always going to lead someone to God?
3. Is science in opposition to religion/God?

Letter 2

Review Questions
1. Why was Screwtape angry with Wormwood?
2. How did Screwtape advise Wormwood to use the Church as a stumbling block?
3. According to Screwtape, why does God allow people to be disappointed as they begin marriage, Christianity, or other endeavors?

Thought Questions
1. Why are old habits a threat to new Christians?
2. What, in your opinion, is the most difficult kind of habit to break?
3. Why are people inclined to discount other Christians because they have flaws?

Letter 3

Review Questions
1. How did Screwtape advise Wormwood to use the patient's relationship with his mother?
2. Why was the "elder brother in the Enemy's story" relevant to Wormwood's patient?
3. To what Biblical story was Screwtape **alluding** in this reference?

Thought Questions
1. Should prayer be concerned with physical or spiritual needs? Both?
2. Why do minor irritations cause so much injury to relationships?

Letter 4

Review Questions
1. What is the purpose of prayer?
2. According to Screwtape, where do humans mentally direct their prayers?
3. Where did Screwtape say humans' minds and gazes should be turned when they pray?

Thought Questions
1. "Whatever their bodies do affects their souls." Explain. Do you agree?
2. Is prayer dependent on feelings? Is Christianity? If so, to what extent?

Letter 5

Review Questions
1. What greater event in history had Wormwood written about?
2. What are the pros of war, according to Screwtape?
3. Where would Screwtape prefer for humans to die?

Thought Questions
1. In your opinion, what effect does war have on people's thoughts of God?
2. Does war change people's personalities or amplify them?
3. Why is suffering an essential part of redemption?

Letter 6

Review Questions
1. Did Screwtape want the patient to be immediately called away to military service?
2. Why was hatred of Germans ineffective, according to Screwtape?
3. What are the three circles of the mind? Where did Screwtape want to keep thoughts of God?

Letter 7

Review Questions
1. Did Screwtape want the patient to be ignorant of Wormwood's existence?
2. What were the pros and cons of the High Command's policy on this subject?
3. Why did Screwtape want the church to be small?
4. Did Screwtape want to drive the patient to pacifism or patriotism? Why?

Thought Questions
1. What do you think is the effect of believing or not believing in devils?
2. Is it possible to believe in devils but not God? If so, how?
3. If you are familiar with it, what would Lewis think about the general philosophy in Star Wars?
4. Is this an age of complacency or extremes?

Letter 8

Review Questions
1. What was the law of undulation?
2. Which served "the Enemy" more, peaks or troughs? Why?
3. What two weapons did the nature of God's plan forbid him to use?

Thought Questions
1. How does the law of undulation manifest itself in your life? Does it?
2. What is the difference between "desiring" and "intending" to do something?

Letter 9

Review Questions
1. How was Wormwood supposed to exploit "trough periods"?
2. Who was the inventor of all healthy, normal pleasures?
3. How did Screwtape tell Wormwood to handle the despairing type? The hopeful type?

Thought Questions

1. Have you ever assumed pleasure was innately bad? When does pleasure become harmful?
2. Why do humans feel superior after they have left a "phase" behind?

Letter 10

Review Questions

1. Who were the patient's new friends? Why were they desirable?
2. With what was the word "Puritanism" associated? Was it a positive association?
3. What were the pros of living a double life, in Screwtape's opinion?

Thought Questions

1. How do you choose the people you try to emulate?
2. "All mortals tend to turn into the thing they are pretending to be." Do you agree?

Letter 11

Review Questions

1. What were the four causes of human laughter?
2. Whose side does each cause of laughter support, according to Screwtape?
3. What did Screwtape say was the best way to use jokes?

Thought Questions

1. Why do people tell jokes?
2. What does it mean to "laugh it off"? Is this a good thing or a bad thing?
3. What is a "sense of humor"? Why do you think it is so highly valued?

Letter 12

Review Questions

1. Why was Screwtape glad the patient still attended church?
2. What, according to Screwtape, makes people reluctant to think about God?
3. Did Screwtape think big or small sins were better for drawing people to Hell?

Thought Questions

1. What are your substitutes for real happiness? Why are they substitutes?
2. Screwtape says, "God is one 'without whom Nothing is strong.'" What does this mean?

Letter 13

Review Questions

1. What offense had Wormwood committed?
2. What mistakes did Screwtape say Wormwood had made?
3. According to Screwtape, what must the patient not be allowed to do next?

Thought Questions

1. How are Satan and God's views of individualism different?
2. How do you choose your tastes? Your friends? Does society play a significant role?

Letter 14

Review Questions
1. To Screwtape, were lavish promises and confident resolutions a good or bad sign?
2. How did the Enemy want men to view their own talents?

Thought Questions
1. What is the true purpose of humility?
2. How should you think about your talents?

Letter 15

Review Questions
1. For what view of time did the Enemy want humans to live (past, present, future, or eternity)?
2. What view of time did Screwtape want man to take?

Thought Questions
1. Do you live in the past, the present, or the future? What does that mean to you?

Letter 16

Review Questions
1. What did Screwtape say were the benefits of church-tasting?
2. What were the characteristics of the other two churches near the patient?
3. What did the two churches have in common?

Thought Questions
1. Is it ever good to be critical of the church? When?
2. How should you differentiate between important and unimportant issues in church doctrine?
3. "The human without scruples should always give in to the human with scruples." Romans 14 says the same thing. What would a practical application of this principle look like?

Letter 17

Review Questions
1. What was gluttony of Delicacy?
2. What was the "All-I-Want" state of mind?

Thought Questions
1. Why is gluttony considered a sin? Who does it hurt?

Letter 18

Review Questions
1. What were the two options that the Enemy offered for human sexuality?
2. What is the role of sex in God's design, according to Screwtape?
3. On what did Screwtape want marriage to be based?

Thought Questions
1. What are appropriate reasons for marriage?
2. An axiom of Hell was, "'To be,' means 'to be in competition.'" Discuss. Do you agree?

3. What does it mean to be "in love"?

Letter 19

Review Questions
1. Why did Screwtape not want Wormwood to share his letters with anyone?
2. What, according to Screwtape, was the cause of Satan's quarrel with God?
3. What kind of uses did Screwtape see for marriage?

Thought Questions
1. Why is God's love so incomprehensible?

Letter 20

Review Questions
1. What type of woman did Screwtape think was appropriate?
2. What two kinds of women did Screwtape believe haunted every man?

Thought Questions
1. How is sexual taste affected by society? What is currently considered attractive?

Letter 21

Review Questions
1. What other condition is needed for men to be angered by misfortune?
2. Why did Screwtape say the claim to own time is absurd?
3. How are the words expressing possession (my, your, our) confusing?

Thought Questions
1. Why do you feel a sense of ownership of your time? What effect does that claim have?

Letter 22

Review Questions
1. With whom had the patient fallen in love?
2. Why did Screwtape call God a hedonist?
3. What two sounds did Screwtape describe as the sounds of Heaven?
4. What happened to Screwtape in the middle of the letter?

Letter 23

Review Questions
1. What was the third power besides the world and the flesh?
2. What advantages did Screwtape see in the idea of a "historical Jesus"?
3. What was the "game" in the sentence, "Only such faith can outlast the death of old cultures and the birth of new civilisations"?

Thought Questions
1. Are all great moral teachers essentially the same? Why or why not?
2. What is the problem with concepts of the Jesus of history today?
3. Does it surprise you to think of the gospels edifying, not making Christians? Do you agree?

Letter 24

Review Questions
1. What was the weak spot in the patient's young woman?
2. Why was it helpful to Screwtape that the patient considered himself equal to his new friends?

Thought Questions
1. "It is always the novice who exaggerates." Why? Do you agree?
2. Have you ever laughed at people who believed differently? What is the danger with that?

Letter 25

Review Questions
1. What is "Christianity And"?
2. According to Screwtape, why was novelty unsatisfying?
3. What was the demonic strategy with regard to the sentiments of a given age?

Thought Questions
1. Why are people afraid of "The Same Old Thing"?

Letter 26

Review Questions
1. How was unselfishness defined differently for men and women?
2. What was the Generous Conflict Illusion?

Thought Questions
1. What does being unselfish mean to you? Why do it?
2. Is it sometimes better to be selfish? Why or why not?

Letter 27

Review Questions
1. How was the patient dealing with distractions? What did Screwtape want him to do?
2. What was the "Heads I win, tails you lose" argument?
3. How is God's perception of time different from humans'?

Thought Questions
1. How do you determine whether someone's words are true?
2. Why are people so unwilling to claim absolutes today?

Letter 28

Review Questions
1. Why did Screwtape not want the patient to die?
2. Why were the young less easy to mold and more willing to die, according to Screwtape?
3. In Screwtape's view, was birth or death more important to God?

Thought Questions
1. How is death viewed today? As natural? As the prime evil?

2. Is it harder to do an extremely difficult thing once or to do a moderately difficult thing daily?

Letter 29

Review Questions
1. What two qualities did Screwtape urge Wormwood to promote in his patient?
2. Of what vice could they not make men proud?
3. What was the risk of making the patient a coward?

Thought Questions
1. "To be greatly and effectively wicked a man needs some virtue." Do you agree? Discuss.
2. Is courage a virtue or simply the "form of every virtue at the testing point"? Why?

Letter 30

Review Questions
1. How had the patient behaved during the first air raid?
2. How did Screwtape differentiate between fatigue and exhaustion? Which did he prefer?
3. The raids provided an opportunity for what emotional attack?

Thought Questions
1. Is it **ironic** that Wormwood would make claims for justice to Screwtape? Why?
2. Do you use "real" to describe emotional or physical facts? Why?

Letter 31

Review Questions
1. What was Wormwood's supreme failure?
2. How did Screwtape describe death?

Thought Questions
1. What is your perception of devils?
2. Is Lewis's picture biblical?
3. If Screwtape wanted to target you, what would be his plan of attack?
4. Is it hard to translate Screwtape's negative message into Lewis's positive one?
5. What is the effect of Lewis's device (speaking in opposites)?

WRITING REFINEMENT:
Using the Vocabulary

Literary terminology can be helpful in identifying the parts of a novel. Since *The Screwtape Letters* is an epistolary novel and slightly different from a typical novel, the traditional parts and roles may be harder to spot. There are several possible answers, so have a good reason for yours. (If you are not sure of the meaning of these terms, look back at "Using the Vocabulary" in the "Writing Refinement" section at the beginning of this book.)

Identify each of the following elements in *The Screwtape Letters*:

Narrator:

Protagonist:

Antagonist:

Plot:

Internal conflict:

External conflict:

Climax:

Looking Back, Looking Forward

Congratulations! You have now worked your way through twenty classic works of British literature. Along the way, you've assembled a variety of reading and thinking tools that will be valuable in future reading and writing experiences. So, you may be thinking, what now?

The Next Step

Almost every author says the key to good writing is lots and lots of reading with all your senses on alert. One goal of this collection is to make you aware of books as books: deliberate creations by human authors—sometimes with a distinct purpose, other times with an unintentional effect.

Thinking about literature in this way should not decrease your ability to simply enjoy a good book. Rather, it should add another dimension to the mystery, romance, thrill, and delight that an author is able to create using a few masterfully placed words on a page.

As you continue to read and write about literature, always remember that you are first and foremost a critic. Books, even the most pleasurable, contain ideas, and it is your job to recognize those ideas and consider their implications. Whether you ultimately reject or accept an author's viewpoint, you cannot help being influenced by it.

For students in ninth to twelfth grade, or for learners of any age who are ready to ask questions and think analytically about literature, a great resource is *The Lost Tools of Writing* from the CiRCE Institute. Using the classical method, this guide will help you remove anxiety from the writing process. This program will build on the skills you've begun to hone and will help you continue your journey through the world of literature.

Perspectives, Take Two

In today's society, mass media has an enormous impact on the way people view the world. Every day a million and one ideas compete for your attention. Most messages are designed to be absorbed passively and accepted without questioning. If nothing else, this book encourages you to practice reading (and, by default, listening and watching) with your brain fully engaged. If you can do this, you will be better prepared to distinguish between that which is merely enjoyable and that which is worthy of application to your own life.

In closing, as you continue this journey, it is worth repeating that participating in the great conversations of literature is an art that takes a lifetime to refine. However, it is an art that will yield a lifetime of fruit as you celebrate with family and friends the joy of laughing, crying, and simply bubbling over with excitement about the great stories which are now yours to share.

Best wishes on your journey!

Photo Credits

The following images have been retrieved from the Library of Congress digital Prints and Photographs collection, unless otherwise noted. The reproduction number follows the photo description.

PAGE 63:
J. Austen, LC-USZ62-103529

PAGE 99:
Charles Dickens, courtesy Wikimedia,
http://upload.wikimedia.org/wikipedia/
commons/0/02/Charles_Dickens_1858.
jpg

PAGE 115:
Mother Teresa, courtesy Wikimedia,
http://upload.wikimedia.org/wikipedia/
commons/7/7f/Mother_Teresa.jpg

PAGES 135 and 147:
C. S. Lewis, courtesy Encyclopedia
Britannica, 82724-050-DE6C50B8
CSLewis_Britannica.jpg

PAGE 141:
J. R. R. Tolkien, LC-USZ62-74760